Music Assessment for Better Ensembles

MUSIC ASSESSMENT
FOR BETTER ENSEMBLES

Brian P. Shaw

OXFORD
UNIVERSITY PRESS

OXFORD
UNIVERSITY PRESS

Oxford University Press is a department of the University of Oxford. It furthers
the University's objective of excellence in research, scholarship, and education
by publishing worldwide. Oxford is a registered trade mark of Oxford University
Press in the UK and certain other countries.

Published in the United States of America by Oxford University Press
198 Madison Avenue, New York, NY 10016, United States of America.

© Oxford University Press 2018

CIP data is on file at the Library of Congress
ISBN 978-0-19-060315-1 (pbk.)
ISBN 978-0-19-060314-4 (hbk.)

9 8 7 6 5 4 3 2 1

Paperback printed by Webcom, Inc., Canada
Hardback printed by Bridgeport National Bindery, Inc., United States of America

For Reid and Mary Claire, who bring me endless joy

CONTENTS

FOREWORD

How music educators map student progress in group and individual instrumental and vocal music education has all too often relied on less-than-rigorous methods and a lack of awareness of the relationship between curriculum and assessment and of ideas that can effectively map progress in diverse student populations. It is for this reason that I was delighted to read Brian Shaw's *Music Assessment for Better Ensembles*, which covers a host of issues related to the application of evidence-based approaches to assessing student progress within music ensemble settings.

By providing thought-provoking examples, Brian Shaw encourages readers to adopt a variety of approaches that focus attention on the purpose of each assessment task and how they relate to learning targets. Most important is the quality of the assessment and the way results are communicated to students to ensure productive, well-focused student learning and motivation. The ten chapters that comprise this book provide easy-to-understand explanations of the rationale for assessment-focused teaching, the symbiotic relationship between assessment and curriculum and how a curriculum can be designed to work for both teachers and students, how to gather information and map student progress, blueprints for assessing a broad range of musical skills and understandings, contextualizing feedback so that it can be used to steer further improvement, grading systems and approaches, and a template for future developments within music education.

Each of these ten chapters encourages music educators to update and redefine their teaching practices using ideas that are well grounded and that advance thinking in music education in profoundly important ways. This is an important contribution to the literature and one that will be of practical value to a host of music educators who wish to ensure the best results from their students.

Gary E. McPherson
Ormond Professor and Director, Melbourne Conservatorium of Music,
University of Melbourne

PREFACE

I did not begin my teaching career expecting to write a book about assessment. As a high school band director, I built rapport, studied my scores, rehearsed my groups, assigned written work mainly when I was being observed, and gave almost everyone an A. My professional life changed forever during my first year as an administrator when Jan, the assistant principal, brought (dragged?) me to an Assessment for Learning workshop with Rick Stiggins. I was hooked. It was immediately clear to me that AfL had *huge* untapped potential for music educators. My bookshelf was soon full of assessment and grading advice, but all of it was for general education. I also had many resources for music teaching, but I was unable to find a music-focused assessment resource that felt right. So, here we are. My hope is to provide ensemble music teachers with the most valuable ideas from the more than two hundred books, articles, and resources that I consulted during the preparation of this book, as well as the years that I have spent developing and using assessment strategies and helping pre-service and practicing teachers do the same.

This book is part exposition and part advocacy. Many music teachers see formal assessment as something extraneous to their "real" work; they only do it because they have to. When approached by administrators or colleagues in other departments, we are habituated to defensively think, "Music is different. Whatever they have to say, it probably doesn't apply." (We don't have time for it anyway; there's a concert coming up!) However, if we have the courage to peer out of our foxholes, we will see that assessment is something that we are already doing in our classrooms and that it can be transformative when used strategically. Whether you are an undergraduate student, a new teacher, or a veteran, I urge you to take your own first steps toward incorporating improved assessment strategies into your teaching. You will surely be happy you did.

The book is divided into three sections. The first addresses foundational concepts underlying a program of Assessment for Learning in ensemble music classrooms. Chapter 1 provides a rationale for assessment-focused teaching and explores several concepts underpinning the approaches found throughout the book. Chapter 2 details the symbiotic relationship between assessment and curriculum and how curriculum can be designed so that it works not only for teachers but for students as well. Chapter 3 lays out the many ways in which teachers can gather information about students' understanding and performance, while Chapter 4 includes suggestions about how to process that information in ways that can inform teaching and learning.

The next section turns to the application of assessment concepts in music classrooms. Chapter 5 contains a blueprint for assessing a broad range of musical understandings and abilities in the ensemble classroom. Chapter 6 is dedicated to fundamental performance skills, while Chapter 7 focuses on using assessment and feedback strategies during concert preparation. The final section of the book deals with grading practices. Chapter 8 contains an overview of how grades are determined and used, and Chapter 9 details grading issues specific to ensemble classes. Finally, Chapter 10 is a call to action for music teachers, including suggested first steps to get started with better assessment and grading.

Each chapter begins with Essential Questions. You may wish to answer these in advance, and update your answers while or after you read. There are also Activities at the end of each chapter, which will hopefully prove useful with connecting ideas in the text to your own vision for and experiences with music education. On page xvi, there is also a self assessment tool, Example 0.1. Just as you might do with students, I encourage you to reflect on your own assessment journey before reading and to return to page xvi regularly, possibly using a different color or shape to represent different stops along your way.

The examples in this book are included primarily to stimulate readers' thinking rather than being immediately usable "off the shelf." I have not attempted to include every assessment that teachers might need. In addition to being impossible, this would also be undesirable. Teachers rail against standardized assessment because it does not acknowledge the diversity of students, teaching philosophies, and contexts that characterize education today. Classroom assessment is more likely to facilitate learning when it is organic, customized, and timely. Thus, these examples are intended for teachers to *adapt*, not necessarily *adopt*. Examples from other disciplines are also useful. We have much to learn from our fellow educators, and we are more successful as a profession when we do.

I have tried to balance the needs and desires of aspiring and practicing teachers with scholarly issues regarding curriculum and assessment. I share the concern that music is sometimes taught and assessed in overly simplistic ways and that most topics are more nuanced than they first appear. I am equally aware of the realities of life for ensemble teachers and the diverse teaching approaches they use. This resource is for all music educators.

Simply using more assessment does not result in student success. Assessment and teaching are inseparable. Assessment is not a Band-Aid that can be slapped on to cure all of our pedagogical ills. An assessment revolution is inevitably a teaching revolution, but it is a revolution that our students deserve.

ACKNOWLEDGMENTS

I am grateful to the many people who helped bring this book to fruition. My superb editor Norm Hirschy has been an encouraging and insightful partner. Those who read drafts, offered valuable feedback, and shared examples with me also have my gratitude. I am further indebted to Gary McPherson for his generous contribution.

This work has been shaped and motivated by the outstanding students, colleagues, administrators, teachers, and mentors that I have been fortunate enough to encounter along the way. It is an honor to have worked with and for so many terrific people. Their voices are implicit in this text. My parents have been supporting my musical endeavors for decades and deserve their own round of applause.

Since our undergraduate days in Bloomington, my wife Julia has been my muse, my coach, my sounding board, my compass, my support system, and my constant companion. This book would not be possible without her.

Columbus, Ohio
July 2018

Example 0.1: Self assessment for music educators

I feel good about the assessment I am doing now.	o 1 2 3 4 5
I can define assessment.	o 1 2 3 4 5
I can explain how assessment usually occurs in music classes.	o 1 2 3 4 5
I can describe the limitations of typical music assessment practices.	o 1 2 3 4 5
I can list the three steps in the assessment process.	o 1 2 3 4 5
I can explain how to balance various types of assessment.	o 1 2 3 4 5
I can explain the Assessment for Learning questions.	o 1 2 3 4 5
I can define KRSPD and explain how it relates to music instruction.	o 1 2 3 4 5
I can create learning targets that serve my curriculum.	o 1 2 3 4 5
I can describe a variety of assessment methods and their strengths.	o 1 2 3 4 5
I can explain characteristics of effective feedback.	o 1 2 3 4 5
I can choose an evaluation method that matches the task and learning target.	o 1 2 3 4 5
I can list a variety of ideas for assessing my students' musical skills.	o 1 2 3 4 5
I can list a variety of ideas for assessing my students' musical performances.	o 1 2 3 4 5
I feel like I can design my own assessment tasks and evaluation tools.	o 1 2 3 4 5
I am ready to take steps toward using more assessment in my classroom.	o 1 2 3 4 5
I feel confident about creating thoughtful grading procedures.	o 1 2 3 4 5
I can explain the difference between assessment and grading.	o 1 2 3 4 5
I understand why traditional music grading practices are controversial.	o 1 2 3 4 5
I can explain how to make grades align with content mastery.	o 1 2 3 4 5
I am excited about assessment and/or grading in my teaching.	o 1 2 3 4 5

SECTION ONE
Foundations

CHAPTER 1

Why Assessment?

The aim of assessment is primarily to *improve* and *educate* student performance, not merely to *audit* it.

Grant Wiggins[1]

Box 1.1: CHAPTER 1 ESSENTIAL QUESTIONS

1. What is assessment? How is assessment helpful to music teachers and music students?
2. How can educational psychology help music teachers use assessment effectively?
3. What tensions are commonly associated with assessment, and how can they be addressed?

BENEFITS OF EFFECTIVE ASSESSMENT PRACTICES IN ENSEMBLE CLASSROOMS

Music educators quickly learn that their musical knowledge and conducting chops don't automatically result in student success and engagement. The ensemble in the teacher's head has technical accuracy, resonant tone, conceptual understanding, tall vowels, tuned instruments, motivation, and confidence. However, the ensemble in the teacher's classroom tends to inhabit a different, messier reality. Each student possesses a unique set of understandings and misunderstandings, technical abilities and inabilities, and beliefs about themselves and their music-making. It is difficult for teachers to stay informed about exactly what their students know and can do. When problems arise, it's often difficult to say how to fix them.

Furthermore, the students themselves often really don't know how well they are doing. When they are aware that they need to improve something, they often don't know how, are afraid to ask, or both. Everyone in the room might be working hard on the music, but something isn't quite adding up.

Assessment is a part of the answer to all of these situations in ensemble classrooms. Assessment can reveal important but previously hidden information about abilities and attitudes to both teachers and students, enabling instruction that is more personal, effective, and empowering. An overwhelming body of educational research suggests that well-used classroom assessment can dramatically improve student achievement.[2] Since research also suggests that lower-achieving and less confident students tend to drop out of music,[3] the case for more frequent, systematic, and thoughtful assessment in music education is compelling. Teachers often grumble about instructional initiatives they perceive as coming from administrators or policymakers, but upgrading classroom assessment practices is different. Assessment is not the "flavor of the month." Assessment is here to stay, and it has enormous potential to transform ensemble music instruction for the better, helping teachers achieve their own musical and educational goals.

Who makes the music?

Music educators in secondary schools have traditionally aimed instruction, assessment, and feedback at groups of students, whether the group is the full ensemble ("You all need to practice this weekend!") or a section ("Tenors! You're rushing!"). Even though the group most often performs together, effective teaching and assessment address what individual students know and can do. A musical ensemble consists of individuals making music simultaneously—correct or not, unified or not. Professional ensembles are not great because of magic; they are great because they are comprised of knowledgeable musicians who do certain identifiable things expertly and poignantly. The way to a better ensemble is to cultivate better individual musicians in the ensemble.

Assessment of individuals can lead to a greater sense of individual responsibility and accountability, a culture of achievement, and ultimately a stronger performance. Most instruction is applicable to many students. Still, music teachers are at their best when they know what each individual can already do, what steps they should take to improve, and whether those steps resulted in progress or not. Assessment facilitates good teaching.

Who needs assessment information?

Assessment guru Rick Wormeli wrote that without assessment teachers are "teaching blind."[4] For ensemble music teachers, information is critical to everyday decisions. How do teachers know what music to choose for their students? How do they know where to begin rehearsals? How do they determine what to say at parent conferences? How do they decide who gets the solo, or moves up to symphony? How do they know what music literacy concepts to teach this year or this week? These decisions should be made on the basis of information about students, combined with the teacher's expertise. The more accurate and specific the information is, the more helpful it is as a component of educational decision-making.

Teachers are not the only participants in education; others also seek and use information about student achievement. Assessment reveals the information students need to know how well they are doing, and what and how to improve. Assessment can provide information to families about ways to support their children's musical growth and offer honest justification for decisions about placements, roles, solos, and honors. Teachers can use assessment information to informally or formally evaluate their instruction and work with colleagues to create coherence across grades or buildings.[5] Assessment can also provide information to school administrators and state officials, signaling that music courses have important course content and demonstrating student growth in mastering it.

Everyone has heard the maxim that knowledge is power. However, not all knowledge is equally powerful. What information students, parents, teachers, and other stakeholders have is more important than how much they have. *Actionable* knowledge is power. More of the right information can lead to more effective teaching and more effective, participatory learning.

MUSIC TEACHERS AND MUSIC STUDENTS

Who teaches school music?

The image of an ensemble music teacher is usually fashioned after musical heroes such as professional and military conductors, whose primary concern is producing a product for the stage rather than the development or welfare of the musicians. There is no more clear illustration of what I call the **Maestro Mentality** than Arturo Toscanini's famous quote to a beleaguered trumpeter: "God tells me how the music should sound, but you stand in the way!" The Maestro says, "It is your job to learn the parts and my job to put them all together." The Maestro decides the interpretation. The Maestro sees student misunderstandings as problems, to be dealt with as efficiently as possible.[6] The Maestro responds to musicians' perceived failures with admonitions about focus, hard work, and traditions of excellence.

Many music teachers, consciously or not, are emulating some version of this model. Yet, if we are to realize ideals such as "Music for every child; every child for music," there will be fundamental differences between what school music teachers do and what professional conductors do. Teachers use their personal musicianship to teach and inspire students and collaboratively make music with them. Teachers understand that students are at various stages in their musical and personal development, seeing students' misunderstandings as normal opportunities for learning. The *performance* is the sole concern of the Maestro professional conductor. While performances are still important in schools, the musical engagement and development of *children* is of primary concern to the school music teacher.

Who participates in school music?

In the American popular imagination, "musical talent" is a special gift that some people have and most people don't. Clichés like "I don't have a musical bone in my body" reinforce the idea that musical ability is genetic and unchangeable. It is widely accepted in our culture that innate gifts or talents are required for success in performing music, despite empirical evidence suggesting that music ability is learned rather than inherited—even abilities like perfect pitch.[7] Still, as in other subjects, assessment in music has historically served to sort and select students rather than facilitating instruction. Students are not only learning about music; they are also learning whether they should continue to pursue it in school. Too often, our assessment practices contribute to the perception that music is not for everyone.

Evolving views of music education

Beliefs about who should be enrolled in music have evolved over the decades, but questions persist about what to do with students who aren't immediately successful. While the Maestro improves the ensemble by encouraging struggling students to *quit*, the teacher improves the ensemble by helping struggling students to *learn*. Contributing ensemble members don't necessarily have private lessons, fancy instruments, or prodigious talents. They can do certain identifiable things. This book will highlight what some of those things are, and how teachers can track students' progress toward their goals.

WHAT IS ASSESSMENT?

Assessment defined

Broadly defined, **assessment** is the evaluation of student learning, progress, or achievement. The three steps in the assessment process are: (1) collecting information about student performance; (2) evaluating the information; and (3) acting accordingly (Figure 1.1).

The word assessment comes from the Latin verb *assidēre*, which translates as "sit beside" or "sit with." For music educators, the teacher assessing a student by "sitting beside" her may conjure images of a piano teacher on the same bench instead of standardized tests. A private teacher sitting beside a student and guiding learning by listening, questioning, modeling, and offering feedback is a good metaphor for assessment practices that benefit students. "Accountability" testing has driven many teachers toward negative feelings about assessment. Others argue that music assessment is futile, since we cannot definitively make value judgments about competing interpretations or whether a person or group "has it." These are not the kinds of appraisals that facilitate teaching and learning. **Classroom assessment** is assessment created or used by teachers as a part of their instruction. As classroom assessment is the kind that benefits students the most, it is the sole focus of this book.

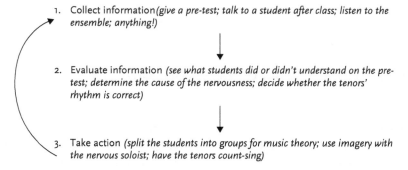

1. Collect information *(give a pre-test; talk to a student after class; listen to the ensemble; anything!)*

2. Evaluate information *(see what students did or didn't understand on the pre-test; determine the cause of the nervousness; decide whether the tenors' rhythm is correct)*

3. Take action *(split the students into groups for music theory; use imagery with the nervous soloist; have the tenors count-sing)*

Figure 1.1: The assessment process

Classroom assessment is not something new to music or music education. In fact, in many school buildings, the music teachers assess students more often than their colleagues in other departments. The purpose of this book is not to encourage music teachers to start using assessment, but to refine and broaden the assessment they are already doing.

The state of the art

Educative assessment is about using information to guide teaching and learning. However, many American music teachers use assessment practices that are less than optimal. We tend to use assessment for judgment rather than improvement. We tend to be long on problems and short on solutions. We fall into the convenience of assessing groups rather than harnessing the power of assessing individuals, and into addressing symptoms (what we're hearing in rehearsals) rather than causes (individual knowledge and fundamentals). Ensemble grades are frequently determined by students' ability to arrive on time for concerts and appear engaged rather than the extent to which they have mastered the course content. This is all understandable. Teachers and even administrators typically have little or no formal preparation for using assessment to advance student learning.[8] Still, music educators who are ready to take steps toward sound assessment and grading practices will be pleased with the results.

Discourse about assessment has become so pervasive that teachers and administrators occasionally forget what it is intended to accomplish. "Doing Assessment" can become a sort of educational performance art, with "I cans" on the walls, technology at the ready, and color-coded charts of student progress ready for sharing in faculty meetings. However, one can be busy Doing Assessment without adopting the fundamental pedagogical changes it implies. As professor Janet Coffey and colleagues write, "The core of formative assessment lies not in what teachers *do* but in what they *see*."[9] Nobody has time to Do Assessment if it doesn't help students learn.

ASSESSMENT AND EDUCATIONAL PSYCHOLOGY

Educational psychology, the study of learners and how they learn, provides insights for effective instruction, assessment, and feedback. Teachers can use principles of educational psychology to help students become better musicians now and better music learners in the future. Successful students have certain patterns of thought and behavior more often than unsuccessful students. Just like musical performance, these thought processes and actions are not inborn. Each can, and should, be taught.

Metacognition

A critical question for learners is whether they are able to "zoom out" from their minute-by-minute learning process and see the big picture. This ability, called **metacognition**, literally means "thinking about thinking," but for students it might best be characterized as "awareness of yourself and your learning." Metacognitive learners are cognizant of their own abilities, preferences, and tendencies; can figure out the requirements of a given task; develop or apply appropriate strategies; set goals and monitor their progress; and use self-regulation to stay on track. It is no surprise that students who use these techniques are typically more successful in school and in music than those who don't. Therefore, savvy teachers are continually promoting and modeling metacognitive strategies with their students. Assessment can help students develop the self-awareness they need to become more capable and independent.

The Zone of Proximal Development

Some tasks are well within a student's current capabilities. Students may be reinforcing what they can already do, but are not learning many new things; for example, a high school cellist playing music from a beginner book. Some tasks are so difficult that a student will not be able to master them anytime soon, even with help, like a beginning cellist playing three-octave scales. The third possibility is students working on something they can *almost* currently do, with a little help; a task that's near their current abilities. These tasks are said to be within the students' **Zone of Proximal Development** (ZPD),[10] represented by Figure 1.2; for example, the beginner cellist learning a new note or the high schooler learning the three-octave scale only after she has mastered the two-octave scale.

As the student's capabilities in a particular area increase, so does the ZPD. New goals, previously unattainable, can become proximal. In the meantime, using knowledge of the learner's current abilities to change task requirements to make them proximal or establish intermediate goals that are proximal is called **scaffolding**.[11] Teacher and student work together through assessment to know what's in the ZPD and what's just outside of it, so that they can determine the student's **Next Steps**: the concrete actions students

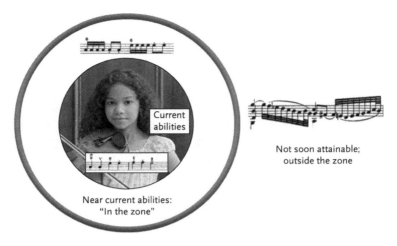

Figure 1.2: The Zone of Proximal Development (ZPD)

should take in order to achieve their immediate goals. Teachers who teach "in the zone"—where each individual's current objectives are not yet attained, but are soon attainable—are setting their students up for confidence and achievement. The process of establishing and supporting individual goals is called **differentiated instruction**. Differentiation—the collaborative negotiation of what goals are "in the zone," and what supports students need to accomplish them—is not possible without detailed knowledge of each learner's abilities, and is a central outcome of classroom assessment.

Self-efficacy

Student performance is affected by many factors beyond "talent" and "effort." Each day, students navigate a struggle to define themselves as they age, an overwhelming desire not to lose face in front of peers, challenging personal situations, and other pressures that influence their abilities and attitudes. Some students are metacognitive about their feelings and attitudes—able, for example, to realize that their anxiety about an upcoming playing test causes them to avoid practicing. Unfortunately, others are less aware of how their feelings and attitudes affect their behavior and school performance. Helping students understand and ultimately control their motivations, emotions, beliefs, and interpersonal interactions is the premise of **social-emotional learning** (SEL). Many educators are excited about SEL in part due to research demonstrating its potential to improve both students' approaches to school and their academic performance.[12]

Although SEL is multifaceted, one important element with implications for assessment is **self-efficacy**. Self-efficacy is a student's perception of the probability of her or his success for a particular task. Self-efficacy influences motivation, persistence, effort, resilience, self-regulation, and embracing challenges.[13] (Notably, all of these attributes are touted as benefits of music instruction.) If students do not believe that they are likely to be successful in a given situation, they will be much less likely to expend the necessary energy and risk failure.

The fact that patterns emerge in the interplay between self-efficacy and behaviors is the basis for psychologist Carol Dweck's landmark concept of two mindsets. A student with a **fixed mindset** tends to believe that intelligence and other abilities are "fixed" within a person: you're born with a certain amount of ability, and you can't do much to change it. Students with fixed mindsets, believing that they cannot change their circumstances, worry whether their talents measure up; their implicit goal (called a **performance goal**) is to prove their abilities to themselves and others in order to receive affirmation or quash self-doubt. The opposite pattern is the **growth mindset**. Students with a growth mindset see intelligence and abilities as malleable: everyone has a starting place, but can work to get better. Students with growth mindsets aren't trying to *prove* their ability; they are trying to *im*prove their ability (a **learning goal**). There is not a strict dichotomy between fixed and growth mindsets, and like self-efficacy they are task-specific. A student may believe that effort improves performance in science but not in choir, or that she can work to improve her range but could never be good at improvisation. (*And, since she'll never succeed anyway, why try?*) Most of this is invisible to a casual observer in a classroom, but the effects of the ways that students approach learning are profound.

Unfortunately, fixed mindsets are endemic in school music. Countless parents have told me that music just wasn't their child's gift, or that they themselves "can't carry a tune in a bucket." When people attribute success or failure to inherited qualities, they are less likely to invest effort, which seems either futile or unnecessary. At the first sign of difficulty, students who see musical ability as fixed may conclude that they are not one of the lucky few who "have what it takes," stop trying as hard, predictably fail to achieve, and drop out of music programs. Others succeed early, conclude that they have special gifts, and then are unable or unwilling to practice or receive instruction when faced with challenges. Teachers who see musical ability as fixed may consciously or subconsciously invest more in certain students,[14] or they may ascribe students' struggles to lack of commitment rather than a need for scaffolding. A central reason to reconsider assessment and grading practices is the powerful message they send to students about whether they are the kind of person who can succeed in music.

Growth mindset has been mischaracterized both as the answer to systemic poverty (especially when couched as "grit") and as an excuse for children to learn nothing as long as they have healthy self-esteem. Growth mindset is not the same as mindfulness, positive thinking, or the self-esteem movement of decades past. Success comes from more than beliefs; it also comes from effective teaching and student involvement. And, of course, growth mindset is not a substitute for achievement; we do want students to eventually succeed. The trouble is that students never succeed when they feel hopeless and quit.

ASSESSMENT DILEMMAS

What's measurable is measured (and treasured)

Value judgments about what and how to measure are inherent in any evaluation. Thus, teachers have the power to dictate how students conceive and complete musical tasks through their assessment criteria. No matter how artistically conceived or democratically intentioned a task may be, students will inevitably structure their efforts to meet the teacher's expectations. If a performance assessment includes only notes, rhythms, and tempo, students will prepare in a certain way. If it also—or only—includes musical expression and stylistic appropriateness, students will prepare differently and teachers will listen differently. Any criteria not measured inevitably receive less attention from teacher and students. Thus, assessment comes to define the task, and by extension the curriculum. This is the embodiment of the maxim that "what's measured is treasured." Even more insidiously, "what's measured" is not random. Choices about what and how to assess are often made based on convenience. What's easily measurable is usually measured, and thus what's measurable is treasured—often without teachers or students realizing it. Students' musical values, and therefore their musical identities, are shaped by the teacher through assessment criteria and practices.[15] Assessment in music education has traditionally emphasized attendance, punctuality, and concert attire, complemented by factual knowledge and basic performance technique. While these elements are straightforward to assess, they are only a fraction of what most music educators hope to offer students, and they paint a monochromatic picture of what it means to "be a musician."

It is worth considering the extent to which competitions and festivals influence what's measured and treasured in rehearsal rooms. If assessments effectively define a task, then judge sheets—arguably the single most widely used music assessment—have defined musical performance as an activity in which correctness is king, dynamics are separate from expressivity, and students' individual abilities and understandings are unimportant. Everyone is familiar with the concept of teaching to the test. Music educators may be teaching to the judge sheet, whether they recognize it or not.

Parts and wholes

Consider a rainbow. Its most characteristic and fascinating quality is that it contains the full spectrum of colors, each subtly blending into the next. In many schools, however, one of the first things that students are taught about rainbows is that they have seven discrete colors. While the rainbow does indeed contain those seven colors, to characterize it this way is **reductionist**: depriving it of its essence and richness through an overly simplistic reduction into components. The typical approach to music performance assessment has been to list a number of musical elements and add up a number of points for each to arrive at a total score. Certainly, no one would argue that any list of categories fully captures what transpires on a stage. As psychologist and testing critic Alfie Kohn wrote, "We miss the forest while counting the trees."[16]

Although musical elements are often presented as being independent of one another, no reasonable musician would deny that tone affects intonation, or that dynamics and balance are closely related. Musical elements are not independent, but rather *inter*dependent. Assessment that presents musical elements as disjoint and unconnected paints them in an unmusical light. And, in the same way that the seven-colored rainbow overlooks the interplay between colors, judge-sheet assessment often overlooks the connections between features of a performance. Musi*cal* assessment highlights the intersections of musical elements and their purpose as enablers of artistic expression. Of course, discrete musical understandings and abilities are important goals of music education and crucial for a satisfying performance. Neither an all-trees nor an all-forest approach will suit teachers' aims or students' interests.

The myth of objectivity

No assessment is truly objective. Numerical scores and official-looking documents tend to have an air of authority, but numbers can be derived as capriciously as any other evaluation. Certain strategies can reduce—but not eliminate—bias and subjectivity, and they cannot remediate hidden bias resulting from decisions about criteria. The same performance evaluated by different people or using different criteria will be evaluated differently, no matter how well crafted the evaluation process may be. As British researcher and assessment expert Caroline Gipps emphasized, "To see assessment as a scientific, objective activity is mistaken. Assessment is not an exact science."[17]

The first step toward dealing with the subjectivity inherent in student assessment is to acknowledge it. Teachers who adopt a defensive posture, attempting to insulate themselves from all possible criticism, are not removing the possibility of bias from the assessment process, but instead turning their attention away from student learning. Decisions about what to evaluate or emphasize inherently tilt the scale toward some students' skill sets and away from others'. Teachers who recognize this, rather than denying it, are well positioned to have fair and informed conversations about assessment and to make better educational decisions based on its results.

Teachers can also reflect on their own potential biases. Implicit (i.e., unintentional but real) bias can be found in many places. It is widely understood that characteristics including gender identity (also in relation to voice part or instrument), race, ethnicity, communication style, sexual orientation, English proficiency, and exceptionality[18] can affect how a predominantly white and middle-class music teaching workforce views students' accomplishments. Less commonly discussed, but still relevant, are appearance and grooming, previous academic or disciplinary history, and musical tastes. An uncomfortable but worthwhile consideration is the extent to which music teachers assess students based on how similar to *us* they are, as musicians, students, and people. Subjectivity exists in both assessor and assessment, and always will.

SUMMARY

While instruction would be easier if students and teachers always had accurate information about abilities, challenges, and ways to improve, this is almost never the case. Assessment is a process of generating useful information to facilitate teaching and learning. Assessment practices in ensemble music classrooms do not always promote the idea that music is something that all children can and should learn. Metacognition, the Zone of Proximal Development, and self-efficacy are foundational concepts for music educators to apply to their assessment and teaching practices.

Assessment is not without controversy. Answers to questions about objectivity, fairness, and musical integrity are important to effective, personal, and artistic music education. Still, assessment has the power to transform students' music learning and experiences.

TERMS

- Maestro Mentality
- Assessment
- Classroom assessment
- Metacognition
- Zone of Proximal Development
- Scaffolding
- Next Steps
- Differentiated instruction
- Social-emotional learning
- Self-efficacy
- Fixed mindset
- Growth mindset
- Performance goals
- Learning goals
- Reductionism

ACTIVITIES

1.1. Define "assessment." Summarize how assessment can be helpful in ensemble music classrooms today and how that is similar to or different from how assessment has historically functioned.

1.2. Observe teachers at work in a variety of situations: classrooms, studios, rehearsal rooms, and the like. Write down only the ways that the teacher sought information about students' abilities. Afterward, review your notes. Reflect on how often this happened, what information the teacher was typically seeking, and any other observations you made about the flow of information in the classroom.

1.3. Describe how have you seen the "What's measured is treasured" phenomenon affect classrooms or other areas of your life. How can it be helpful and how can it be harmful?

1.4. Make a list of common occurrences in music or other classrooms that might promote growth mindset and learning goals, as well as those that promote fixed mindset and performance goals. Which is the most common? Does it appear that teachers you have had are aware of the difference, even if they didn't know the terms?

1.5. Reflect on your own knowledge about and experiences with assessment. What are you most hoping to learn from this book? Are you apprehensive about anything?

CHAPTER 2

Assessment and Curriculum

Being busy does not always mean real work. . . . There must be forethought, system, planning, intelligence, and honest purpose, as well as perspiration. Seeming to do is not doing.

Thomas Edison

Box 2.1: CHAPTER 2 ESSENTIAL QUESTIONS

1. How is curriculum related to assessment?
2. What are learning targets, and how can their use benefit students?
3. What are the five types of learning targets, and how do they inform teachers' thinking about assessment?

CURRICULUM BASICS

The Latin term **curriculum** means the "course to be run": a blueprint for what students will do and learn in a program of study. There are two approaches for determining what to include in a curriculum. The teacher can fashion a sequence of familiar lessons, pieces, warm-ups, and activities, or begin with goals and then design educational experiences to help students achieve them.[1] Championed early by Jerome Bruner, the latter approach is termed **backwards design** in Grant Wiggins and Jay McTighe's landmark book *Understanding by Design*.[2] It is the educational application of the axiom "Begin with the end in mind." Only after educators have determined what students should know and be able to do can they determine what to teach and how to teach it. Things that students should know or be able to do as a result of their education are called **outcomes**. Basic outcomes might include naming the parts of the instrument, using solfège for diatonic patterns, or fluency with a list of scales. Educators may desire myriad other outcomes, such as affective engagement, leadership development, or a lifelong interest in music.

Outcomes are often based on **standards**, which are lists of goals that are typically published by states and professional organizations. One example from the recent NAfME Music Standards is for students to "select varied musical works to present based on interest, knowledge, technical skill, and context."[3] Another example from the Virginia Music Standards of Learning reads "The student will sing expressively . . . consistently using facial and physical expressions that reflect the mood and style of the music."[4] These and other standards describe outcomes in general terms, but details are usually left unstated. Educators need to **unpack** standards, melding the standards' broad aims and individual students' backgrounds and interests into the specific goals most appropriate for their own classrooms. Once outcomes have been clarified, the next step is to decide what constitutes **evidence of mastery** (also called **success criteria**) for each. Each standard will have several associated outcomes, and each outcome usually has multiple indicators of success.

The process of identifying precise learning goals involves probing the implicit understandings held by teachers. Many would agree that students in an orchestra classroom should learn to read music. However, a collaborative process of determining evidence of mastery for "reading music" would soon reveal that it means different things to different people, and so it is with technique, listening, interpretation, creativity, and everything else. As the old saying goes, "The devil is in the details." It is only with clear knowledge of *what* to assess that decisions about *how* to assess can be made.

LEARNING TARGETS

Even if teachers have clearly defined student outcomes and evidence of mastery, they may not have done so in a way that is easily comprehensible by the learners themselves. Using an archery metaphor, Jan Chappuis and her colleagues at the Assessment Training Institute wrote, "Students can hit any target they can see and holds still for them."[5] Students can "see the target" when the teacher frames learning goals so that students can easily understand them. Outcomes written for *students* are called **learning targets**. A common way to create learning targets is to construct them in a way that reinforces the students' understanding of, and involvement in, their own learning: "*I can . . .*" or "*I can . . . this means . . .*" or "*I can . . . so that . . .*" An example might be "I can read the Level 1 rhythms. This means that I can clap and count rhythms containing quarter notes, quarter rests, and pairs of eighth notes in ♩, ♩, and ♩ time while keeping a steady beat."

Traditional curriculum writing has focused more on teachers and teaching than on students. Even in classrooms with detailed curricula, the exact ways in which the concepts will be experienced and assessed are often not made explicit. It is frequently assumed that once a certain level of granularity is reached (for example, "Teach students to count basic rhythms"), the teacher intuitively knows what the unpacked targets will be. More specificity enables students to "see" the target by clarifying exactly what they should be able to do and guaranteeing that the target holds still for them over the course of a unit, semester, or year. When students aren't clear about what they are trying to achieve, the teacher has to do all of the work. Educators are familiar with the benefits of consistent expectations for classroom routines and behavior. Consistent expectations for learning and understanding are at least as important.

The "clear target" approach is not without drawbacks. Clear targets can be limiting. Imagine a composition project with clear guidelines such as being eight measures long, diatonic in the key of G or D, using rhythms from this list, having antecedent/consequent phrases, and so on. The process of discovery and novelty has been removed; students are more likely to "paint by numbers" than to compose something creative or expressive. Advanced students who have hit a common target might be less motivated to continue pushing themselves. Finally, clear targets can be reductionist (see Chapter 1). These challenges can be addressed through including the big picture in learning targets, using differentiated instruction to set goals that challenge students, and considering how to balance teacher direction and student self-determination in each learning experience.

Ensemble music is usually taught in a **spiral curriculum**. While math students may sequentially learn to calculate the area of a square before moving on to circles, ensemble teachers do not have the luxury of teaching rhythms for the Fall Concert and delaying notes until the Winter Concert. The spiral describes a cycle of revisiting the same concepts in increasing depth with each piece and concert as the students' Zones of Proximal Development expand. When returning to familiar content, it makes sense to use familiar objectives and assessments. Fifth-grade string students can work to achieve the target of "I can play my instrument with good tone" even though it's impossible for them to be ready for the San Francisco Symphony by the end of the year. Their standard for success can be a tone that is developmentally appropriate for fifth graders, even though next year's standard of what "play my instrument with good tone" means will be different. Teachers may wish to explicitly reinforce this concept with students: even though they are successful fifth graders, there is more work to be done. Using intermediate proximal learning targets helps to celebrate each step students take toward mastery, rather than emphasizing how far they are from All-State.

WRITING LEARNING TARGETS

The process of constructing learning targets involves turning the specifics of the curriculum into detailed, concrete outcomes that are easily digestible by students. A few examples of learning targets are in box 2.2.

Box 2.2: SAMPLE LEARNING TARGETS

- I can carefully assemble my instrument so that I am ready to play my best.
- I can identify opportunities for dynamic contrast. This means that I can look at a piece of music and identify the places where the music is loudest and softest, as well as places where the dynamics should change rapidly or gradually.
- I can accurately sing a major scale using solfège syllables and Curwen hand signs. This will help me to sing music just by reading the notes.
- I can follow a conductor. This means that I can play using the tempo that the conductor indicates with his or her gestures, start and stop when I'm supposed to, and get louder or softer when the conductor shows it. This helps our ensemble play together and make adjustments during performances.

Box 2.3: GUIDELINES FOR WRITING LEARNING TARGETS

1. The target should use language that is easily understandable by the student.
2. The target should be aimed at individual students.
3. The target should address learning outcomes, not activities.
4. The target should describe *one* thing that can be assessed.
5. The target should be something that nearly all students can reasonably expect to achieve in the near future.

While there is no formula for all learning goals, box 2.3 contains several guiding principles.

Guideline 1: Student-friendly language

For some music educators, writing learning targets for students involves a new way of conceptualizing student achievement. Often, musicians value minutiae, complexity, and abstraction outside the ZPDs of their students. However, using **student-friendly language** is *not* oversimplification or "dumbing it down." Students deserve the full benefit of their teachers' musical knowledge, but they also deserve a teacher who communicates in a clear and straightforward manner. Music educators need to explain complicated jargon, concepts, techniques, and affects in a way that is comprehensible to younger students and those who struggle with language in a way that is not dumbed down, but rather artfully conceived. Students often struggle to connect discrete skills to the broader musical enterprise. Embedding the larger principle into the target ensures that the connection is made. Table 2.1 is a list of "sentence starters" that may aid in varying the ways in which learning targets are conceived and phrased, while maintaining a focus on understandability.

Guideline 2: Individual focus

If instruction and assessment are to be aimed at individual students (as described in Chapter 1), then learning targets should be crafted so that

Table 2.1: LEARNING TARGET STEMS

Targets	Explanations
I can . . .	This means . . .
By Friday, I should be able to . . .	All that means is . . .
We are learning to . . .	By . . .
	In order to do that, I need to be able to . . .
	I will have to apply my knowledge of / ability to . . .
	Because . . .
	If we didn't, then . . .
	That will help me to . . .
	Musicians _____ so that . . .

it is clear to students that they alone must master them. If the teacher frames the goal as "We will sound good playing the run before Letter C," a student lacking confidence may be accustomed to thinking, "Other people are better than I am; I'll fake it and not play; we'll sound good; everybody wins." Since many students (and indeed teachers) in ensemble music are accustomed to group-oriented thinking about student performance, the individual accountability of the "I can . . . " archetype is a powerful construction.

Guideline 3: Outcome focus

Doing an activity or exercise such as Solfège Knockout or air bowing is not a learning goal, and thus is not a subject of a learning target. The focus of a learning target is learning that students will acquire or demonstrate during the course of the activity. Accordingly, teachers may wish to avoid "I can play Solfège Knockout" and instead use "I can sight-sing diatonic pitch patterns beginning on *sol* or *do*." Similarly, learning is not the same as avoiding mistakes. Learning targets are best crafted with affirmative rather than negative language: "I can sing it accurately" in place of "I can sing it without errors."

Guideline 4: Assessable (active) focus

Learning targets may involve understanding or factual knowledge. However, knowledge and understanding are difficult even to define, let alone assess. Students need to do something to demonstrate that they know something; how else can the teacher determine what they know? A learning target containing inactive verbs such as "know" or "understand" is not yet fully unpacked. Students will be able to hit the target most often if, for example, they know that what the teacher means by "understand phrasing" is drawing arcs indicating phrase structure above a familiar musical line. Table 2.3 lists common verbs that specify how students will actively demonstrate their learning. Additionally, learning targets communicate expectations most clearly when they contain only one type of outcome. There is no disadvantage to breaking up a multifaceted learning target into multiple discrete ones, especially since the "This means . . . " section can clarify how the targets are interdependent.

Guideline 5: Short-term focus

Not every skill or understanding can reasonably be achieved in a single class or lesson segment. Students' spirits are lifted, and their self-efficacy is increased, by *accomplishing* goals. Teachers may choose to reframe a long-term target as a series of intermediate targets that students can hit in succession. Each time a new target is hit, the students' Zone of Proximal Development has grown. The next target, previously outside of the ZPD, is then attainable. For example, if a chorus teacher has a learning target for the beginners about reading pitch patterns using all of the notes of the diatonic scale, his students are unlikely to be able to hit the target in the near term. To promote a sense of achievement and momentum, this teacher might instead have a series of learning targets in an appropriate sequence: "I can sight-sing unfamiliar pitch patterns beginning on *sol* and using *sol* and *mi*." "I can sight-sing unfamiliar pitch patterns beginning on *sol* and using *sol, mi,* and *do*." "I can sight-sing unfamiliar pitch patterns beginning on *sol* and using *sol, mi, re,* and *do*."

Table 2.2 contains potential missteps and solutions for writing learning targets. Again, there is no universal formula.

ENABLING SKILLS

After teachers have crafted their learning targets, the next step is to carefully consider what knowledge or skills students will need in order to hit each target. Music performance is full of simultaneous, multilayered processes. If the learning target at hand is "I can play 'Aura Lee' with correct notes and rhythms," and the new note for this exercise is a C♯, it is possible to overlook everything besides the C♯ that students need to know and be able to do in order to hit the target: assemble the instrument, read the rhythms, and so on. These are collectively called **enabling skills**: skills without which the task at hand will be difficult or impossible to do correctly. A list of enabling skills is an excellent way to craft the "this means . . . " section of a learning target, helping students understand what it means to "sing expressively" or "sight-read."

Whether the students are beginners or advanced high school musicians, the wise teacher always has enabling skills in mind. In keeping with backwards design, the teacher might ask: "What do students need to be able to do in order to be successful with today's material? What are the ways a student might (or probably *will*) get this wrong?" It is easy

Table 2.2: IMPROVING LEARNING TARGETS

Problematic target	Explanation	Improved target
"I can understand that the melody is the most important musical line."	"Understanding" is inactive and abstract. The target should be something active and concrete.	"I can explain how *melody* is related to *balance* in an ensemble."
"Students will master the chromatic scale."	Does not say what students will do. Does not show students the target.	"I can play a one-octave chromatic scale from memory in quarter notes at MM=80."
"I can play the one-octave concert B♭ scale from memory in quarter notes at MM=80 without stopping or mistakes."	Does not use affirmative language; focused on errors.	"I can play the one-octave concert B♭ scale from memory in quarter notes at MM=80 with correct notes and a steady tempo."
"Students will identify the intonation idiosyncrasies and necessary adjustments in fingerings or positions for the notes most commonly needing adjustment for his/her instrument."	Language overly complex. Meaning potentially unclear to students.	"I can explain which notes are most commonly out of tune on my instrument and what I should do to keep them in tune."
"I can sing expressively."	Musical jargon. Meaning potentially unclear to students.	"I can sing expressively. This means that I can use my facial expression and body language to communicate the meaning of the text."
"I can sing a major scale and write it on the staff."	Two outcomes in one. Singing and writing are not the same thing.	"I can sing a major scale in solfège." "I can write a major scale on the staff using accidentals and key signatures."
"I can sing warm-ups using the Five Vowels."	Focused on the *doing* of an activity, not the *learning*.	"I can sing the Five Vowels, 'oo,' 'ee,' 'eh,' 'ah,' and 'oh,' using the correct shape for each."

to focus on the new material of the day without ensuring that each student is positioned to process or implement it. This is one of the sharpest contrasts between professional conductors and school music teachers on the podium. The Maestro says, "My job is to say that it should sound like this. Your job is to be able to figure out how to do it on your own." The educator says, "Here's the goal. We have to do a lot of things to get there! Let's go through this one step at a time." The authors of *Understanding by Design* weren't specifically describing music teachers in this passage, but they may as well have been:

> We find that many teachers overlook the enabling skills at the heart of long-term successful performance. . . . Far too often it is *assumed* that students will somehow already possess key enabling skills . . . with the predictable results that cause more educators to complain about the absence of those skills than to target them in their planning.[6]

Any set of enabling skills is a list of potential student misunderstandings or skill deficits: the bow may be too close to the bridge, or the student may not understand that a tie means "add these two note durations together and don't tongue in between." In fact, given the experience level of a typical student, it is almost certain that some enabling skills will require reinforcement. Rather than beginning a lesson or unit with advanced concepts (which are usually a synthesis of enabling skills) and then working to remediate deficits with those skills, the shrewd teacher ensures that students have mastered each enabler before attempting to apply them. Students who are asked to integrate skills or understandings they do not possess are being set up to fail. The wise teacher sets students up to succeed.

TYPES OF LEARNING TARGETS (KRSPD)

Musical concepts tend to be complex and multifaceted, and evidence of mastery can take many different forms. Consider the example of dynamics. A student who is proficient in dynamics might be expected to define "dynamics" and "dynamic contrast," perform a *crescendo* and a *decrescendo* in tune on a single pitch, rank dynamic markings from softest to loudest, and be able to identify the peaks and valleys in a piece of music—and these are only a fraction of the possibilities. Not surprisingly, a system for categorizing learning targets is helpful.

There are many ways to classify student outcomes. Educational goals are frequently divided into two major categories: knowledge and skills. To differentiate between the possession and application of knowledge, this is also sometimes described as "KUD" (Know—Understand—can

Do). Teachers may also recognize the cognitive processes in Benjamin Bloom's revised Taxonomy: Remembering, Understanding, Applying, Analyzing, Evaluating, and Creating. While these and other systems are useful, the system we will use in this book comes from Jan Chappuis and colleagues: Knowledge (factual and conceptual understandings), Reasoning (thought processes), Skills (psychomotor abilities), Products (student creations), and Dispositions (attitudes and affective states).[7] Abbreviated KRSPD, these **learning target types** are detailed later in this chapter.

If one conceives of a concept as a sculpture, learning target types are analogous to viewing the same sculpture from different angles. Just as one can view a sculpture from the front, back, or sides, every musical concept has elements that one must know, understand, and be able to do. The question is not whether a particular type of learning target is somehow applicable to a given concept—it almost certainly is—but, given limited class time for instruction and assessment, which types of learning targets will be the best angles from which teachers can see if students mastered the objectives. It is often desirable to examine student achievement from multiple angles, which can be done in a single assessment or across several assessments as the situation warrants.

One commonly used way of differentiating between learning target types is by examining the main verb used in the target. If the target is "I can *list* reasons that good posture helps my singing," it is a Knowledge target, and "I can *sing* with good posture," is a Skill target. Table 2.3 contains verbs typically associated with each type of target. While verbs can be useful, the intent of a learning target is more important than its verb. Some verbs can be misleading. A student can *know* that music is often organized into large sections that sometimes repeat (Knowledge), *know* how to use form to guide interpretation (Reasoning), or *know* how to use form in a composition project (Products). Schools are full of ambiguous verbs: *know,*

Table 2.3: COMMON VERBS FOR LEARNING TARGETS

Knowledge	Reasoning	Skills	Products	Dispositions
• Define	• Summarize	• Sing	• Design	• Value
• Describe	• Analyze	• Play	• Develop	• Appreciate
• List	• Problem-solve	• Buzz or bow	• Create	• Feel
• Label	• Predict	• Demonstrate	• Compose	• Embrace
• Recognize	• Evaluate	• Clap and count	• Improvise	• Be
• Identify	• Compare	• Sight-read	• Plan	• Exemplify
• Explain	• Infer	• Perform	• Innovate	• Experience

understand, memorize, synthesize, comprehend. To maintain an active focus, teachers can phrase learning targets in a way that students can easily understand what they will be expected to do.

Knowledge targets

Knowledge is comprised of three subcategories: factual knowledge, conceptual knowledge, and procedural knowledge.[8] **Factual knowledge** is the ability to recall or list declarative facts—for example, this note on the staff is D, or the string bass sounds an octave lower than the written pitch. **Conceptual knowledge** is connection or explanation of facts—for example, how balance involves relationships both within and between sections in the ensemble. **Procedural knowledge** encompasses steps involved in doing something, like how to acknowledge applause and exit the stage. More examples of musical Knowledge include:

- Recognizing articulation markings (*factual*)
- Knowing how many beats a note gets (*factual*)
- Understanding relationships between dynamic makings (*conceptual*)
- Explaining how scales and key signatures are similar and different, and why students learn them (*conceptual*)
- Explaining the connections between categories on a judge's sheet (*conceptual*)
- Listing the characteristics of a good breath (*procedural*)
- Using a key signature to find *do* or the tonal center (*procedural*)
- Assembling an instrument (*procedural*)

Knowledge outcomes might be phrased as learning targets like this:

Recognizing articulation markings
- I can recognize the articulation markings *staccato, legato, marcato, tenuto,* and *accent* and say what they mean in English.

Explaining the connections between categories on a judge's sheet
- I can explain how each category on the Solo & Ensemble judge's sheet relates to the others.

Assembling an instrument
- I can explain and complete all of the steps of assembling my instrument so that I can play my best.

Reasoning targets

Reasoning targets involve students applying critical thinking skills to musical situations. Reasoning can build on Knowledge, but it can also motivate students to acquire and refine it by providing a context and a "need to know."[9]
Examples of musical Reasoning could be:

- Grappling with dilemmas and questions without easy answers
- Critiquing a concert recording
- Asking why composers made certain musical decisions

Reasoning outcomes might be phrased as learning targets like this:

Grappling with dilemmas
- I can reason through difficult questions. This means that I consider different facts and arguments before arriving at a clear position that I can defend with specifics.

Critiquing a concert recording
- I can watch or listen to music I have played and evaluate the performance.

Asking why composers made certain musical decisions
- I can use my musical and contextual knowledge to infer why composers wrote music the way that they did.

Skill targets

Skill targets involve real-time execution of psychomotor abilities: the intersection between thoughts and movements. Skills in KRSPD are not "thinking skills," which are Reasoning targets, and they do not include "knowing how" to do things, which would be classified as procedural Knowledge. Skills are the active *doing*: moving, playing, singing, clapping, and dancing. In a music classroom, examples of Skills could be:

- Singing or playing with good tone quality
- Holding a bow or instrument
- Singing or playing a scale or technical exercise
- Reading rhythms or pitches
- Performing a passage with interpretation/expression
- Performing a piece

Skill outcomes might be phrased as learning targets like this:

Holding a bow or instrument
- I can play with a proper bow hold. This means that all of my fingers are curved and where they're supposed to be, and that my grip is both firm and relaxed, so I can sound my best.

Performing a passage with interpretation/expression
- I can sing expressively. This means that I can use phrasing, facial expressions, and body language to convey the mood of the music and the meaning of the text.

Performing a piece
- I can perform my part for *Pomp and Circumstance* with technical accuracy and ensemble unity.

Product targets

Product targets involve the application of other abilities to generate a finished, tangible result. Product targets help answer the persistent student question: "When am I going to have to use this?" Products are often categorized as authentic assessment, which is described in Chapter 3.

Examples of Products could be:

- Compositions and improvisations
- Program notes
- Performance, song, or album reviews
- Planning and giving individual performances

Product outcomes might be phrased as learning targets like this:

Compositions or improvisations
- I can create music that I like listening to.

Program notes
- I can use my musical and contextual knowledge to write program notes for the music that we're playing.

Performance, song, or album reviews
- I can write like a music critic. This means that I can state a nuanced opinion, support my opinion with specific details, make comparisons to similar musical works, and communicate clearly to a nonexpert audience.

Disposition targets

Many **Disposition** targets fall into one of three categories. One is social-emotional learning (SEL), including being confident when performing or feeling capable of musical improvement through practice. The second category involves attitudes, such as open-mindedness, enjoyment of music, or respect for others. A third category, particularly salient in a music class, is affective response or musical engagement—as a performer, creator, or listener. More examples of Dispositions could be:

- Having an aesthetic experience creating, listening, or performing
- Appreciating unfamiliar musical genres
- Feeling a sense of belonging in an ensemble or program
- Embracing challenges with no immediate solution
- Wanting to continue singing after high school

Disposition outcomes might be phrased as learning targets like this:

Having an aesthetic experience making music
- I can feel emotionally connected to the music I'm making.

Appreciating unfamiliar musical genres
- I can keep an open mind while I'm learning to appreciate unfamiliar kinds of music.

Embracing problems with no immediate solution
- I can embrace challenges that will take a long time to address. This means that I can keep working even if I don't feel like I'm an expert right away.

ALIGNING INSTRUCTION AND ASSESSMENT WITH LEARNING TARGETS

The benefits of learning targets are realized when there is coherence between the curriculum, learning targets, instruction, and assessment. Teachers are generally excellent at communicating what students are supposed to be doing, but are often less concerned with communicating what the results of the "doing" will be: what the students are supposed to be *learning*. Students who know the desired understandings or improvements from a particular lesson or run-through can work actively and independently to accomplish their goals.

Many schools currently require learning targets to be displayed in classrooms, but the fact that targets are in the room does not ensure that students can "see" (i.e., understand and internalize) them, or that the teacher and students are working to achieve them. This is not a critique of displaying lesson objectives; it is a reminder to not "post and forget" learning targets. To point students in the direction of the target at the beginning of a unit or lesson is a positive step; to continually use formative assessment and foster explicit connections between activities and targets (e.g., "Take thirty seconds to talk with your section about why we are learning this") is even better.

Upfront learning targets require modification in constructivist instructional paradigms, including discovery learning and project-based learning. In these approaches, educators do not specify objectives in advance, preferring to co-construct them with students as the class unfolds. Teachers may also intentionally not reveal some learning targets at the beginning of a lesson, preferring to guide students to discover the desired understandings for themselves. For example, rather than "covering" the concept of balance, the teacher might engage students in *uncovering* principles of balance through questions and experiences, only naming the term afterward. Inspired teaching using mystery and intrigue to stimulate the discovery process is hampered by too much advance detail. Still, in these calculated learning experiences, the teacher usually has certain objectives in mind, which are ultimately made clear to students. Learning targets are not intended to limit teacher creativity or to foreclose possibilities for serendipitous growth.

Mastery is multidimensional, and mastery of one dimension does not necessarily indicate mastery of another. Skills are (and should be) a mainstay of the ensemble music experience, but if only Skills are being assessed, teachers may assume that students have mastered other elements of the curriculum when they have not. Knowledge, Reasoning, Skills, Products, and Dispositions all work together to build a complete picture of students' abilities. Any assessment will provide information, but the right assessment of the right target will yield the best information for supporting teaching and learning. Armed with a set of clear learning targets that students can "see," the teacher is ready to move on to the next step: collecting information about the extent to which each student has hit each target.

SUMMARY

Effective teaching and assessment require teachers to have a clear idea of what their students should know and be able to do, and students need this information as well. The process of creating learning targets involves transforming the teacher's curricula and expectations into statements that are specific, actionable, and understandable to students. The KRSPD framework acknowledges that there are many different ways of being successful with music, each providing an essential piece of the puzzle. KRSPD can also help to illuminate under-addressed areas for teaching and assessment.

TERMS

- Curriculum
- Backwards design
- Outcomes
- Standards
- Unpacking
- Evidence of mastery
- Success criteria
- Learning targets
- "I can . . . this means . . . "
- Spiral curriculum
- Student-friendly language
- Enabling skills
- Learning target types
- Knowledge
- Factual knowledge
- Conceptual knowledge
- Procedural knowledge
- Reasoning
- Skills
- Products
- Dispositions

ACTIVITIES

2.1. Choose any broad musical concept: singing, dynamics, listening, etc. Write at least one learning target for each type in the KRSPD framework.

2.2. Choose one abstract musical concept, such as phrasing, timbre, or blend. Write how you would explain this concept to (1) college music majors; (2) high school students who had been in music classes for several years; and (3) beginners in sixth grade.

2.3. Think of common music teacher instructions to students, possibly from your own teaching, that communicate what students should merely be doing. Write how these instructions could be rephrased to also communicate what students should be learning.

2.4. Make a list of three to five broad aims of music education. Elaborate how assessment could inform you whether your students are achieving these goals.

CHAPTER 3

Gathering Information

Collecting information doesn't require tests, and sharing that information doesn't require grades.

Alfie Kohn[1]

Box 3.1: CHAPTER 3 ESSENTIAL QUESTIONS

1. What different kinds of assessment are there, and how can they work together?
2. What is validity, and how can teachers ensure that assessments are valid?
3. What are common strategies for gathering information, and when is each most effective?
4. How can assessment function in an inclusive music classroom?

ASSESSMENT VOCABULARY

The word "assessment" is used so often that its meaning has become ambiguous. Assessment includes any evaluation of student learning, progress, or achievement. **Grading** involves teachers recording a quantitative value to report achievement to colleges, parents, and others. Grades are normally based on assessment, but assessment does not necessarily affect students' grades. In fact, a strong case can be made for ungraded assessment as the most beneficial kind. The word **testing** can also have multiple meanings, but it most often refers to external, standardized, statewide multiple-choice evaluations. (Students' music learning, not "accountability," is the purpose of the assessment practices in this book.) In addition, some conceive of assessments as written activities like quizzes, tests, and term papers. While these are all assessments, they only represent a fraction of what assessment can be. Chapter 1 described three steps in the assessment cycle: gathering information, evaluating it, and taking an educational action. These steps can occur at any point in the learning process, which is reflected in the three **assessment types**: diagnostic assessment, formative assessment, and summative assessment.

Diagnostic assessment

Diagnostic assessment happens at the beginning of a school term or before a unit of study and is commonly called a **pre-test**. The purpose of a diagnostic assessment is to acquire baseline performance data so that the teacher can use differentiated instruction: knowing what to teach and to whom. Diagnostic assessment enables teachers to set achievement goals tailored to a class or individual student, and can later be used as a reference to judge how much progress has been made.

Formative assessment

While diagnostic assessment takes place prior to a unit of study, **formative assessment** takes place during a unit of study. While "formative assessment" has taken on myriad definitions, it usually refers to assessment conducted during the learning process to help students learn. Assessment researchers Paul Black and Dylan Wiliam provided this description:

> The first priority in [formative assessment's] design and practice is to serve the purpose of promoting students' learning. This distinguishes it from any assessment designed primarily to serve the purposes of determining accountability, ranking, or competence. An assessment activity can promote learning if it provides information that can be used, either by teachers or their students when assessing themselves and each other, to modify the teaching and learning activities in which they are engaged.[2]

As it is intentionally broadly worded, many instructional practices fall under this definition, including routine classroom activities such as instructional questions, exit tickets, and practice problems. Rehearsals and private lessons, where the purpose is improvement rather than demonstration of abilities, also represent formative assessment. Many analogies exist for formative assessment, including a cook's tasting spoon and a checkup at the doctor.

Summative assessment

Rather than serving to guide in-progress learning, **summative assessment** (also called a **post-test**) measures the extent to which a student has achieved a learning goal, often near the end a unit of study. According to education professors Tom Guskey and Lee Ann Jung, "Summative assessments provide teachers with culminating evidence that helps them decide if students have mastered certain content and skills, achieved specific standards, and/or are ready to move on to the next level of learning."[3] Whereas the message from formative assessment might be "Next time you sing this, focus on your intonation," the message from summative assessment might be "The biggest reason you weren't placed in Chamber Choir was your intonation." Unsurprisingly, summative assessment is the type most associated with grading.

In courses that have sequential or cumulative curricula, summative assessment is relatively organic. It feels natural to summatively assess students' mastery of geology before starting a new unit on outer space. Since ensembles use a spiral curriculum for most core course content, summative assessment in music can feel awkward. Summative assessment in ensembles is most often prompted by changes in repertoire or the school calendar, rather than the conclusion of students' engagement with a particular topic. Even if there is a unit on a concept like ensemble blend, blend doesn't become less relevant when the unit ends.

Balanced assessment

Diagnostic, formative, and summative assessment all play a role in the classroom, and there are not always clear distinctions between them. The use of an assessment activity or evaluation tool, rather than its design, determines whether it is diagnostic, formative, or summative. For example, a summative assessment such as a final exam could also provide formative feedback to be used in the upcoming term. The same rubric could be used in formative evaluation of a draft paper and for summative assessment of the finished product.

Table 3.1: ASSESSMENT TYPES

Assessment type	Timing	Purpose	Examples
Diagnostic	Before the learning process	Establish a baseline	Pre-test New student interview
Formative	During the learning process	Guide the learning process	Everyday rehearsal interaction Worksheet or practice quiz Draft of a paper
Summative	After the learning process	Evaluate how much was learned Make recommendations for the future	Audition Term paper Standardized test

Summative assessment can be an important part of the learning process. An upcoming test can prompt students to recall and synthesize information, and growth can result from effort on a paper, project, or performance that might not otherwise have been made. However, only formative assessment provides day-to-day guidance for student learning. Diagnostic assessment is useful because it provides information about where students *started*, but does not shed any light on where they *are*. Summative assessment illuminates where students *ended up*, but often after it is too late to make adjustments. Learning can occur without summative assessment, but not without formative assessment. In the presence of effective formative assessment, summative assessment should not reveal much new information. Furthermore, as its purpose is to prove one's abilities, summative assessment engenders performance goals. Teachers who believe in growth mindsets and want the focus to be on *improvement* may emphasize learning-goal-oriented formative assessment in their instruction.

Figure 3.1 represents how diagnostic, formative, and summative assessment relate to curriculum and instruction for a unit or concert cycle. The teacher considers her outcomes and learning targets and crafts a diagnostic assessment to determine students' initial capabilities. She determines what appropriate intermediate targets are within her students' ZPDs and begins her teaching there. She integrates ongoing formative assessment into her instruction so that she knows what to teach. The unit or concert cycle ends with a summative assessment, and the teacher uses the results to arrive at new learning goals for the next unit or concert.

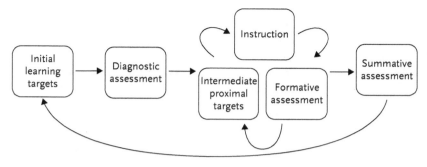

Figure 3.1: Assessment cycle

Formal and informal assessment

An assessment is a **formal assessment** if it feels like an assessment to the students, such as a quiz, audition, or portfolio review. **Informal assessment** is assessment that takes place within the context of routine instruction, when students are less conscious that they are being assessed: practice problems, before-class conversations, regular rehearsals, and the like. Formal assessment tends to yield more precise information, particularly at the individual level. Students may also be motivated to do their best when they are aware that they are being evaluated. However, students and teachers can also gain information from assessment that is done more subtly. Savvy teachers make frequent use of both formal and informal assessment throughout the learning process to inform their teaching.

Diagnostic, formative, and summative assessments could all be formal or informal, resulting in six ways to implement assessment (table 3.2). While it is possible to envision informal summative assessment in a seminar-type course, summative assessment in K–12 education is generally formal. Formal summative assessment is what many people envision when they hear the word "assessment." It has merits, but only as one element of a comprehensive assessment system. Informal diagnostic and formative assessment also has advantages and disadvantages. It may be easy to use informal assessment to obtain information quickly, but without careful planning the information gained may be insufficiently individual, specific, or comprehensive. Informal formative assessment is often the bulk of the assessment that happens in music classrooms. For many ensemble teachers, increasing the frequency and breadth of formal diagnostic and formative assessment of individual students is an initial step that yields tangible benefits.

Table 3.2: SIX WAYS TO IMPLEMENT ASSESSMENT

	Informal	Formal
Diagnostic	Examples: teacher listens to ensemble reading through a new piece; students journal what they know about an upcoming topic. Best used for: quickly understanding generalities about many students' abilities Limitations: can be imprecise and insufficient	Example: anything called a "pre-test" Best used for: helping teachers and students understand students' abilities at the beginning of a year, unit, or piece Limitations: requires advance planning on the part of the teacher
Formative	Example: rehearsal feedback Best used for: all-around good complement to other types Limitations: runs the risk of overlooking some students or concepts if it is the only type of assessment used	Examples: students listen to a rehearsal recording and complete the Listening Log; students turn in an exit slip on the way out of class; the teacher evaluates students in rehearsal using a checklist. Best used for: any situation where specific information about student performance would be helpful to the teacher or student Limitations: requires advance planning on the part of the teacher
Summative	Example: assigning a participation grade based on casual impressions of student behavior Best used for: not recommended Limitations: fairness; accuracy	Examples: Solo & Ensemble performance in front of the class for a grade; written questions or sight-reading for the final exam Best used for: reporting on the big picture Limitations: does not inherently promote learning; students are often unable to use results for improvement; promotes performance goals when overused.

ASSESSMENT FOR LEARNING

Summative assessment is sometimes described as assessment *of* learning—assessment that is used for evaluative and reporting purposes. In contrast, the purpose of **Assessment *for* Learning** (AfL) is to support, rather than report, student learning. Thus, it is the type of assessment that deserves primary attention from educators. While Assessment for Learning and formative assessment are often used synonymously, AfL refers to a continuous program of formative assessment rather than a single event. As Guskey wrote, "To become an integral part of the instructional process, assessments cannot be a one-shot, 'do-or-die' experience for students. Instead, assessments must be part of an ongoing effort to help students learn."[4] Rather than being an add-on to existing procedures, Assessment for Learning is inseparable from instruction.

A requisite element of AfL is that students must be active participants in the learning process; rather than assessment being done *to* students, assessment should be done *with* students. While students are ultimately in charge of their own learning, often the reason students don't succeed is that they do not know what or how to improve. Instruction that helps students answer the three **Assessment for Learning questions** can guide students through the learning process without doing the thinking for them.[5]

Box 3.2: ASSESSMENT FOR LEARNING: THREE STUDENT QUESTIONS

1. "Where am I going?"
   - Ensure that students "see" the relevant learning targets.
   - Break tasks down into components.
   - Involve students in determining why exemplars are successful or unsuccessful.
2. "Where am I now?"
   - Provide students with regular formative feedback.
   - Engage students in self and peer assessment.
   - Return to exemplars for comparison.
3. "How do I get there?"
   - Offer students specific action steps for improvement ("Next Steps").
   - Have students suggest Next Steps for themselves and others.
   - Promote belief in eventual success.

Learning happens most easily in supportive, low-stakes settings, and so does Assessment for Learning. Teachers can lower the stakes in the classroom by responding to inability and misunderstanding with kindness, patience, and nonjudgmental feedback. The purpose of AfL is to enable students to see how to get where they're going while minimizing the doubts and negative self-talk associated with the failures that are a natural and unavoidable part of the learning process. As AfL innovator Rick Stiggins wrote, "Students must not be wondering *if* they will succeed—only *when* they will succeed."[6] Students often perform beneath their true abilities when the pressure is on or when they fear looking clueless or inept, especially in front of peers. The setting in which assessment occurs may be as important as the assessment strategy being implemented. Pop quizzes, surprise playing tests, trick questions, chair challenges, and the like do not reflect AfL philosophy.

VALID ASSESSMENTS

Good information is necessary for helpful feedback and sound judgments. A **valid** assessment is one that allows users to make sound educational decisions based on its results. If an assessment doesn't accurately reveal the right information, then it is ineffective, no matter how precise, detailed, or engaging it might be. Validity is the result of alignment between the assessment and its intended learning targets. There is no universally valid assessment. Assessments could be valid in some situations but not others, according to how effectively and efficiently they yield actionable information about student progress or mastery.

There is often a trade-off between an assessment's convenience and its validity. Using an assessment task that is similar to a real-world application of a goal is called **authentic assessment**. Such tasks are nearly always Product or Skill learning targets. Authentic assessment is desirable—and valid—in many situations. Authentic tasks involve application rather than direct assessment of enabling skills, and often take a long time to complete. Well-designed authentic assessments facilitate growth as well as evaluating it. As Grant Wiggins wrote, assessments "should teach, not just measure."[7] Completing an exam might not "teach" during the course of the assessment, but the process of completing one of these authentic tasks probably will.

If the purpose of an assessment is to determine whether a student has accomplished a goal, there are two ways it can be invalid: **false positive** results and **false negative** results (table 3.3). Aligning the assessment method with the learning target increases validity, but all assessment methods have some risk of misrepresenting student achievement. Teachers are wise to treat all assessments like weather forecasts—they are useful and often correct, but they are wrong frequently enough to be viewed with healthy skepticism. No single assessment can be definitive, but a pattern of assessment results gives teacher and students a basis for drawing conclusions about student performance. Another validity concern

Box 3.3: AUTHENTIC MUSIC ASSESSMENT TASKS

- Selecting, learning, and performing a solo, art song, or pop song
- Composing, notating, and performing original material
- Arranging and performing a familiar tune or using it as a basis for theme and variations
- Teaching a lesson or leading a sectional
- Planning and implementing a performance for relatives or at a nursing home or hospital
- Making an instructional video on some aspect of music or technique
- Integrating music with other artistic and academic disciplines
- A universe of potential ideas developed collaboratively with students

Table 3.3: VALIDITY CHECK

	False negative	False positive
Teacher question	"How could a student do poorly if she actually is capable?"	"How could a student do well if she actually is incapable?"
Examples	She knew the answer but filled in the wrong bubble	She didn't know the answer but guessed correctly
	She could sing it but had stage fright in front of the class.	She doesn't understand key signatures and plays everything in D Major, but the sight-reading was in D Major.
	She knew the answers but didn't finish before the time limit.	She copied the homework.
Possible remedies	Isolate 1–2 learning targets per assessment, and eliminate extraneous steps and requirements.	Incorporate possible misunderstandings when designing assessments.
	Establish a low-pressure environment so that students are less worried about mistakes.	Vary assessment tasks and methods
	Ensure familiarity with tasks and formats.	Establish an ungraded low-pressure environment for formative assessment, so that students feel less pressure to copy work or conceal their weaknesses.
	Ensure that exceptionalities do not disrupt a student's ability to demonstrate musicianship.	Design summative assessments that are not copyable.

is inclusion, which is discussed later in this chapter. All students should have an equal opportunity to demonstrate that they have accomplished the learning goals.

A consideration for validity is **task familiarity**, or the degree to which students are familiar with the procedures they will use during the assessment. When the teaching and testing are too closely aligned, the results are unclear because the assessment mostly evaluates the students' ability to complete the exam. On the other hand, if a student assigned an unfamiliar task (e.g., clapping rhythms with a metronome) is unsuccessful, the results are also unclear. It could be that the student has not met the learning target (reading rhythms) or that the student can read rhythms but is struggling with the particulars of the task (staying with the metronome). In this case, there is a **confounder** present—a condition that makes it impossible to tell whether the student's performance is due to content mastery or the assessment format. Confounders are ever-present in classroom assessment. Teacher-student relationships, nervousness, and misunderstood questions, expectations, and directions all influence results. There is a tradition of secrecy surrounding assessments, but secrecy can compromise validity by increasing the likelihood of misunderstood questions and directions.[8] It may also be the case that, like the metronome, the confounder is actually an overlooked enabling skill of the learning target itself, or a separate but related target worthy of instruction.

If a student does not demonstrate competence with a particular task, the obvious goal is improvement and eventual mastery. This means allowing or requiring students to eventually hit the target through revising, retaking, or redoing assessment tasks. Allowing retakes and redos is an essential component of Assessment for Learning and growth mindsets. There is limited value in giving feedback and hoping for the best. If redos are not necessary, the message to struggling students is either that the task is not very important or that the teacher does not care whether they ever succeed.

A critical distinction for assessors is whether an ability or trait is directly observable. Valid assessment of observable abilities like hand position or vocal range is relatively straightforward. Unobservable abilities such as tone quality or leadership can only be evaluated indirectly through observable criteria. Observables are features of the underlying concept but are usually an incomplete representation. This is particularly true when, as is usually the case, assessors select only certain criteria for evaluation. In a world of complexity and nuance, even a good observable measure is inadequate for making judgments about the broader attribute. There can be no definitive assessment of, for example, "musical ability," because there is no single *thing* called "musical ability." There is grave danger in implicitly or explicitly allowing assessments and grades to be misinterpreted as evaluations of broader traits like intelligence, musical aptitude, responsibility, and motivation. Students and parents frequently attach significance and finality to assessment and grades, inhibiting the learning process by pushing students toward performance goals rather than learning goals. Teachers can make assessment results valid for more users by explicitly reporting what they mean and what they don't mean, and focusing their efforts on achievement rather than aptitude.

ASSESSMENT METHODS

Whereas I have used the term "assessment types" to distinguish between diagnostic, formative, and summative uses, **assessment methods** will refer to the ways in which teachers and students gather information about student performance. Assessment methods generally fall into seven groups: selected response, written response, verbal response, performance or demonstration, personal communication, portfolios, and what I call quick formative assessment techniques (Table 3.4). There is no need to split hairs about the classification of assessment methods, and they are often combined even during a single activity. Any assessment method could be used to gather information about any learning target type, but each method is better suited to certain targets than others. Therefore, teachers must identify and classify learning targets before selecting an assessment method. Identifying methods first (e.g., "Let's have a playing test at the end of the quarter," or "I want my students to write at least once a week") and figuring out learning targets later invites mismatched and therefore inefficient assessment practices.

Most assessment methods could be formal or informal, and formative or summative. Recall that assessment is more about information than any particular teaching maneuvers. Simple observation and other less-flashy but time-honored techniques can also help to establish a knowledge base for making educational decisions. Sometimes, attempts to Do Formative Assessment with a limited number of techniques result in unintentional curricular change when the focus is limited to certain types of learning targets.[9]

The quality of an assessment method is limited by the quality of the task with which it is used.[10] The task generates the student response, and the assessment method captures it. Even a good evaluation tool is limited by a task that does not bring the intended learning into sharp relief. Effective assessment depends on questions and tasks that highlight the most salient features of the issue at hand. Teachers must decide in advance

Table 3.4: ASSESSMENT (INFORMATION GATHERING) METHODS

Method	Examples	Best for ...
Selected response	True/false	Knowledge
	Multiple choice	Dispositions
	Matching	
Written response	Fill in the blank	Knowledge
	Short answer	Reasoning
	Essay	Dispositions
Verbal response	Share answers	Reasoning
	Class discussion	Dispositions
	Oral presentation	
Performance or demonstration	Clapping or counting	Skills
	Singing or playing	Products
	Dancing or marching	
Personal communication	Conferences	Dispositions
	Journaling	Reasoning
	Letter writing	
Portfolio	Portfolio with written reflection	All
	Portfolio conference	
Quick formative assessment techniques (QFATs)	"Fist to five"	All
	Classroom clickers	
	Exit tickets	
Self and peer assessment	Nearly any assessment method	All

whether they want all students to demonstrate the same knowledge and abilities (e.g., a test) or whether there is more flexibility (e.g., open-ended projects). In many assessment situations, the particulars of completion are not as important as the knowledge learners should display. For example, students completing a concert critique could be encouraged to choose from a partial or complete "judge sheet" evaluation, a "Dear composer" letter detailing the group's progress, or a plan for a sectional rehearsal. Providing multiple assessment options is a way to encourage student ownership, facilitate differentiation, discourage copying, keep assessment fresh and interesting, and avoid the "what's measurable is treasured" trap.

Selected response

Selected response involves the students selecting from teacher-created answers. These "closed-ended" assessments include true/false, multiple choice, and matching. Selected response is unsuited for divergent thinking or creative problem solving, and an overreliance on selected response assessments may inadvertently discourage these important pursuits. Still, their ease of completion and evaluation makes selected response questions an indispensable part of the assessors' toolbox.

Selected-response assessment appears to be easy to generate, but it requires thoughtfulness in order to be effective. Incorrect answer choices for multiple-choice questions, called **distractors**, must be carefully written to reflect the most common ways students might misunderstand the question. With successful distractors, incorrect answers lead directly to the feedback the student needs. For example, a teacher might be able to say, "If you chose letter A, you probably need to consider . . ." Distractors should all be plausible. Implausible distractors increase the chances of a false positive. (This is not to say that students do not appreciate an occasional humorous test question or response.) Distractors should also be distinct from one another. Incorrect responses to questions that combine choices (including "B and D" or "All of these") do not reveal the exact misunderstanding; thus, the meaning of the results is unclear. Matching activities can be valid when there are more possible answers than questions, or when answers are used multiple times.[11] True/false questions are less helpful, as there is a high probability of false positives through guessing and because incorrect responses do not provide information about the source of the misunderstanding.

Written response

Written response assessments involve students writing or typing words, sentences, note names, or the like. Written response questions can range in open-endedness from "The trumpet and tuba are ____ instruments" to "What would you say to someone thinking about joining choir?" Often, prompts have as much impact on student responses as what students know. Questions using active verbs such as those in Table 2.3 enhance validity by clarifying the nature of the desired response. A foundational issue with written response assessment is how much detail is enough. One approach is to ask a question two times: "Explain what articulation is to someone who's never heard of it before," and "Now explain what you know about articulation for the Underground Society of Articulation Superfans' biweekly newsletter." Playful response formats such as haikus, limericks, restroom graffiti, tweets, hashtags, parables, "Dear diary" entries, invented musical notation or terminology, and more can keep students engaged while still meaningfully demonstrating content understanding.

Because writing is critical to written responses, students who write well are at risk of false positives. A lengthy or impressive-sounding essay can lack insight or fail to demonstrate content mastery. Conversely, students who are less proficient at writing could possess the desired musical understanding even if its written expression is wanting. If the teacher seeks to understand students' mastery of music content, then including English mechanics dilutes and confounds the evaluation. All too often, written response assessments measure students' writing ability more than their musical ability. This advantages some students and disadvantages others. English usage can be addressed without being scored.

Verbal response

A **verbal response** assessment is one in which students provide their answers orally. Verbal responses include instructional questioning, partner sharing, class discussions, and formal presentations. In the context of cooperative learning, when many or all students have to answer the question, verbal response can provide meaningful opportunities for formative assessment. However, the traditional "call on someone" method only generates assessment information for one student. Often, the teacher asks a question; a section leader raises her hand and answers correctly; the teacher praises the correct answer and moves on. The teacher may have a general sense that "the class" understands but has no information about most of the students.

This problem is especially acute with volunteers. Many music teachers are "hand raisers," but countless astute students are not. In addition, students almost never volunteer when they do not know the answer. Plenty of students never volunteer and feel no accountability for the content. A system of randomization keeps students on their toes and ensures that the teacher is not calling on certain students (such as males or extroverts) more often, which regularly happens without our knowledge. Student names can be written on tongue depressors or index cards and randomly drawn. The teacher could discreetly "stack the deck" to ensure that a particular question goes to a student who has special needs or to avoid selecting a student who dominates conversations. Technology tools can also facilitate randomization. Replacing drawn names helps to ensure ongoing accountability. If names are not replaced, student may feel they are "off the hook" after they have answered. Still, "call on someone" responses are not the most efficient tools for gathering information about many students. Class discussion, which is different from "call on someone," is valuable in its own right.

Performance or demonstration

The **performance** or **demonstration** method is for activities that occur in real time. Musical Skill targets are most naturally assessed as demonstrations. Many music educators have grown accustomed to the "judge's sheet" method of evaluating performances, where every performance is evaluated by every possible criterion. Abandoning the judge's sheet and structuring the performance task and its appraisal according to a select few learning targets enables the teacher to save time by only requiring short passages. It is intuitive that performance would be a primary assessment method in ensemble music. However, since performance is not a natural way to evaluate many critical facets of musicianship, it cannot be the *only* assessment method.

Personal communication

Personal communication can be more intimate, nuanced, and meaningful than other assessment methods. Traditional parent-teacher conferences are an opportunity for appraisal and dialogue, but there are also other formats. In person, over the phone, or through email, even a brief conversation with a student or family member can be heartfelt and honest in a way that in-class interaction does not allow. Music teachers likely do this already. Asking, "Hey, are you getting frustrated with that solo?" after class can generate information that aids teaching. Similarly, journaling and "Dear student" and "Dear teacher" letter writing offer private narrative communication that is often impossible using other assessment methods. Personal communication is underutilized in ensemble music education, and integrates assessment with building rapport.[12]

Portfolio

A **portfolio** is "a collection of artifacts put together to tell a story."[13] Portfolios can produce powerful and revealing chronicles of how students have grown and where they still have room to grow. The advent of easy audio and video recording and storage enables a music portfolio to include not only written work and assessments but also singing or playing, face-the-camera video testimonials, interviews with friends and family, and the like. Portfolios are attractive as an opportunity for sincere student choice in assessment. Teachers may wish to differentiate between process portfolios, or evidence of students' growth over the course of a term, and product portfolios, collections of students' best finished work.

The possibilities for what to include in a portfolio are limitless. Portfolios generally have three components: work samples or other artifacts, written or oral description of each artifact, and a reflective component detailing why the student chose this artifact in particular and what it means for the student's past, present, or future. A music educator wishing to utilize portfolios would be wise to carefully specify what is to be included at the beginning of a course and regularly promote and facilitate artifact collection and storage. To ensure that the descriptive components are appropriate, the teacher may provide students with sentence stems or a reflection form. Portfolio sharing at parent conferences, performances, Board meetings, awards nights, and the like can be compelling.

Quick formative assessment techniques

Quick formative assessment techniques (QFATs) are ways that teachers can collect information or check for understanding without disrupting their instructional flow. The teacher may simply want to know "Do they understand what I just said?" or "Which concepts would students most like to review?" QFATs can produce more helpful answers to questions like "Are there any questions?" "Does that make sense?" or "Are there any spots in the music that you would like to do again?" by prompting all students to answer.

Common QFATs are listed in table 3.5, although there are endless possibilities. Some of them offer information about specific students, such as "Which students can coherently summarize what an interpretation is?" Others only "take the temperature of the room" in the aggregate, such as "How many students selected the correct definition of interpretation?" Instructional technology can facilitate rapid collection and display of students' responses. As the name implies, these strategies are unsuitable as a basis for summative judgments about students' abilities. Nonetheless, they are vital tools for blending formative assessment with instruction. Teachers must decide if they will trust students' self-reports (as in Traffic Light) or desire firsthand evidence (as in short answers). Students may give a thumbs up when they don't understand that they don't understand. Technology is a powerful way to use QFATs and can facilitate all of the strategies in table 3.5.

Table 3.5: QUICK FORMATIVE ASSESSMENT TECHNIQUES

Technique	Description	Sample prompts
Quick rating scales	Students indicate how well they understand or can do something by pointing their thumbs up, down, or sideways, or using the "fist to five" rating scale of 0 (fist) to 5 (five fingers).	"How did we do with our intonation on the B♭?" "How is your memorization of the text to this piece?"
Traffic light	Similar to quick rating scales. Students have red, yellow, and green cards (or cards with ☺, ☻, and ☹, or other emojis) that they can hold up to communicate self-assessment.	"We're almost finished with small-group time; are we ready to come back to the full ensemble?" "How are you feeling about the Level 1 rhythm cards? How about Level 2?"
Exit tickets	Before leaving the classroom, students answer a single question to check for understanding, or write one question they have about the day's lesson.	"What's one question you still have about balance?" "Write a definition of diction and why choirs care about it." "Compose a tweet of up to 280 characters or less about where we should start tomorrow's rehearsal, and why. Use a hashtag (#) to indicate which category of the judge's sheet is most appropriate, such as #rhythms."
Summaries	Students write either a one-sentence summary or a one-minute essay about a concept or topic.	"You have 60 seconds to write a summary of our discussion for a hypothetical classmate who wasn't here." "Explain 'balance' in one sentence."
Short text answers	Students answer a question by writing a word or phrase on a sticky note and posting it in a common place.	"What's one thing you will personally focus on while you're singing at the concert?" "If Bobby Bassist finds that he has poor tone quality when he plays on his open strings, what's something he might try to make his sound better?"
Multiple-choice questions	Students have cards of different colors or shapes, and hold up the card that corresponds with their answer.	"Here's a picture of an interval. Hold up your blue card if you think it's a fourth, your red card if you think it's a fifth, or your white card if you think it's a sixth." "Here's a picture of an interval. Text 'A' if you think it's a fourth . . ."
The Scrambler	Students complete any brief formative assessment activity on paper, then "scramble" themselves to find a new seat with a partner and compare and discuss answers.	"Take your One-Sentence Summary with you to a seat in a different row, and find a partner who plays a different instrument. Read each other's summaries. Are they correct? Are they the same? Be ready to share interesting differences or things you learned with the class."

Engaging students in the assessment process can provide them with more frequent and varied evaluation, and it can also improve their own understandings as they apply relevant concepts and terminology. The ability to critically reflect on one's performance and determine a course of action is fundamental to the musical independence that so many teachers champion. Accordingly, many teachers incorporate **self assessment**, evaluation of one's own performance or progress, and **peer assessment**, evaluation of the progress or performance of a classmate or classmates, into their AfL plans.

Nearly any assessment method can be adapted for self or peer assessment. Students often need support and structure with their initial attempts, but with practice and guidance they can become insightful assessors. At times, students are better positioned than the teacher to provide assessment and feedback to peers. Students are often aware of how those around them perform, what questions they whisper, and what makes them feel insecure. In instrumental classrooms, advanced students may have more knowledge about technique on instruments with which the teacher is less familiar. As experienced teachers know, feedback is frequently more meaningful when it comes from a classmate, and the knowledge of impending peer evaluation is a significant incentive to do good work.

Self and peer assessment promotes and leverages students' knowledge about their own progress and abilities. While teaching students to be effective evaluators requires instructional time, the dividends of metacognition, leadership, and ownership make the investment worthwhile. Teachers report that one of the biggest hurdles to individual assessment in music classes is instructional time. Self and peer assessment can provide efficient and meaningful feedback *and* foster a metacognitive approach to music that enables students to self-correct in the future.

A metacognitive self assessment strategy is for students to report on their own work as they are completing it. An "I don't know" or "Help!" option in a selected response assessment provides more information to the teacher than an incorrect answer, particularly when students are encouraged to detail their confusion. Teachers may also ask students to submit a brief narrative along with a Skill or Product assessment, summarizing the students' appraisal of both the process and the product. This helps teachers know what questions students have or what feedback will be most helpful. In Assessment for Learning, the student is encouraged to discuss and address, not conceal, misunderstandings and possibilities for improvement. Students can also use self assessment to stimulate metacognition for themselves and provide valuable information for their teacher after an assessment, as in Example 3.1.

Example 3.1: Written test debrief

Adapted from Rick Wormeli, *The Collected Writings (So Far) of Rick Wormeli* (Westerville, OH: Association for Middle Level Education, 2013)

Question	Target	Correct		Incorrect		
		Knew it	Just guessed	Made a careless error	I really don't understand this!	Explanation:
1	Durations in simple meter					
2	Durations in simple meter					
3	Durations in compound meter					
4	Durations in compound meter					

Example 3.2: Performance test debrief

Measures	What's hard about these measures?	Nailed it		I'm not there yet			What and how I will practice
		Knew it	Got lucky	Made a careless error	I really can't sing this!	Details:	
1-2							
3-6							
7-8							

ASSESSMENT AND INCLUSION

For legal and moral reasons, students with special needs deserve educators' best efforts to differentiate instruction and assessment. There is no formula that will apply to all students. Many students can be successful with all course content; for others, curricular modifications may be appropriate. Confounders are even more of a concern when assessing exceptional learners. Frequently, tailoring assessment to a particular student does not involve exempting the student from the assessment, but rather altering it: beginning with the learning target, considering various definitions of mastery, and working to enable the student to demonstrate what he or she can do. When differentiating assessment, both content and format deserve consideration. For students with disabilities, several modifications may be helpful, depending on the student's needs. These include shorter assessments (fewer

Box 3.4: SAMPLE STEPS TO INTRODUCE SELF AND PEER ASSESSMENT OF MUSICAL PERFORMANCE

1. Teacher selects three anonymous recorded exemplars representing high, low, and medium achievement on the same familiar exercise or musical excerpt. The teacher could also include a humorous "very bad" fourth example, but in addition to, not in place of, the instructive real example of low achievement.
2. Teacher plays the recorded exemplars for students and asks them to describe each in detail.
3. Students and teacher work together to group the evaluative words to determine criteria. Teacher informs students that they will be creating a system to answer the three AfL questions: "Where am I going?" "Where am I now?" "How can I get there?"
4. Using the criteria they have identified, students re-evaluate the exemplars with attention to each criterion individually or in small groups. Their task is to define what constitutes success with each criterion.
5. Students arrive at common success criteria. They now know "where they are going."
6. Students refer to each exemplar, describing "where they are" in relation to "where they are going." Teacher and students compare and synthesize answers.
7. If desired, teacher and students co-construct rubric indicators (see Chapter 4).
8. Finally, students describe "how to get there" for the exemplars, suggesting ways that the performer in each exemplar might improve his or her performance and relevant practice strategies.
9. Teacher compiles student comments. Students review exemplar comments in pairs or as a class to reflect on the evaluation process and to see if there is a pattern in the feedback they are providing.
10. Students complete a reflection in which they relate the exemplars to their own performance, either on the same excerpt or in general. The reflections could be structured as a journal so that they can make comparisons with the past and set goals for the future.
11. Repeat, vary, and deepen this procedure as students gain experience. Engage students in offering rehearsal diagnosis and prescription.

items per learning target), slower (or faster) pace, assessment methods or question types better suited to the student, removing distractions from the written page or classroom environment, and ensuring that the assessment directions are clear and procedures are familiar.

Students who are English-language learners (ELLs) may benefit from differentiation due to language demands, but language barriers are often misperceived as a lack of musical understanding or general intelligence. Since academic and technical language typically develop later than conversational language, ELLs may be challenged by terminology, writing-intensive formats, and text memorization. Alternate evidence of mastery or different assignment requirements may be situationally appropriate. Teachers can also allow students to complete some assessments in their native languages. It is easy and stimulating for teachers (and native-English-speaking peers!) to learn translations of common musical vocabulary, and students and families always appreciate the gesture.

It is critical to scrupulously follow IEPs, Section 504 plans, and other documented accommodations. Exceptional learners usually have a Teacher of Record or case manager who can collaborate on a best course of action. The books *Teaching Music to Students with Special Needs: A Label-Free Approach*[14] and *Grading Exceptional and Struggling Learners*[15] may also prove useful.

SUMMARY

There are many ways to categorize assessment: diagnostic, formative, and summative; formal and informal; authentic. Combining these with the KRSPD framework and varied assessment methods creates a universe of possibilities for gathering information on students' progress. The teacher's task is to purposefully design and implement elements from all of these categories and frameworks in order to capture specific and relevant information about student learning and performance. Assessment for Learning is incorporating formative assessment into instruction so that students know where they're going, where they are, and how to get there.

TERMS

- Grading
- Testing
- Assessment types
- Diagnostic assessment
- Pre-test
- Formative assessment
- Summative assessment
- Post-test

- Formal assessment
- Informal assessment
- Assessment for Learning (AfL)
- Assessment for Learning questions
- Validity
- Authentic assessment
- False negative
- False positive
- Task familiarity
- Confounder
- Assessment methods
- Selected response
- Distractor
- Written response
- Verbal response
- Performance/demonstration
- Personal communication
- Portfolio
- Quick formative assessment techniques (QFATs)
- Self assessment
- Peer assessment

ACTIVITIES

3.1. Choose a recent class that you took, taught, or observed. (This could be the same class from Activity 1.2.) Make a list of the assessments you remember from the class. Categorize each as formal or informal; diagnostic, formative, or summative; and according to KRSPD. What patterns do you observe? How does assessment align with your other perceptions of the course?

3.2. From your own experience as a student or teacher, list a few examples of situations in which assessments provided false positive or false negative results. How could the assessments have been structured differently to provide better information?

3.3. Write your vision of authentic assessment in an ensemble music class. How do you define a "real musician" for your students? What do "real musicians" do? What are some ways to assess these abilities or dispositions?

3.4. Select an appropriate learning target, and write at least three selected-response questions that would help you gauge students' Knowledge or Understanding. Develop distractors for each question that illustrate probable misunderstandings and partial understandings.

3.5. Think of a class that you took where Assessment for Learning did not seem to be on the teacher's mind. Describe the assessment procedures that were used. How did it feel to be a student in this class? In what ways might AfL be beneficial in this class?

CHAPTER 4

Evaluation and Feedback

Words open up communication, whereas numbers close it down.

Ken O'Connor[1]

Box 4.1: CHAPTER 4 ESSENTIAL QUESTIONS

1. What makes assessment results meaningful?
2. How can teachers structure feedback so that is as helpful as possible?
3. What techniques do teachers use for evaluating student work, and when is each most effective?
4. Which aspects of traditional classroom evaluation deserve reconsideration?
5. When is data useful in a classroom, and when is it not?

By itself, data from an assessment is useless. In order to be meaningful, information requires context. In order to be helpful, it must be presented to a learner in a way that is understandable and designed to facilitate growth.

EVALUATION BASICS

Even with scrupulous attention to design, no assessment is truly objective. As described in Chapter 1, which questions teachers include on a quiz, whether tempo counts the same as note accuracy, and each teacher's intuition about what constitutes "consistent intonation" could all lead to the same student achievement being evaluated differently. "Objectivity" is not necessary for educational decision-making. Teachers should never sacrifice validity or usefulness in a futile quest for objectivity.

Referencing

Assessments that are **criterion-referenced** involve evaluating students against a fixed standard, such as whether they know the fingering for C♯ or can correctly identify these six tempo markings. In contrast, **norm-referenced** assessments judge students against each other, such as audition rankings or grading on a curve. Criterion referencing is clearly the more educative approach. If learning is the goal, who hit the target and who didn't matters more than who won and who lost. Complicating matters is the fact that, in assessment of music performance, literal criteria are difficult or impossible to establish. What counts as "almost always" exhibiting dynamic contrast relative to "sometimes"? Accordingly, performance evaluation often involves **construct-referenced** assessment: the criteria are "constructed" from the evaluator's experience.

Precision

In order for assessment results to be meaningful, they must be viewed in the same way as public opinion polls: there is a margin of error. The margin of error exists because the "true" result is difficult to pinpoint. Grade point averages (GPAs) and national tests suffer from the same limitation. Scores of 35 and 27 on the ACT may represent a meaningful difference, but 27 and 25 do not. A student who got a 27 could have just as easily gotten a 25 if she couldn't sleep the night before, panicked, sat next to the air vent and was freezing cold, or any number of other possibilities. The margin of error in classroom assessment is usually unknown, but we can assume it is substantial. Each assessment provides only a single imperfect snapshot of student performance. Rather than drawing conclusions from any single result, teachers can instead look for patterns of achievement over time.

Levels

The ways that assessments classify student performance are called **levels**. Assessments could have two levels ("yes" or "no"), or as many as 101 (as with percentages). There is no "right" number of levels for an assessment provided that there are meaningful, describable differences between each. Using at least two levels, but not more than four or five, allows the teacher to clearly define the distinctions between each level. This leads to results that are more understandable to students, useful for instruction, and reliable. A **reliable** assessment has consistency of measurement: the same level of accomplishment would consistently receive the same evaluation.

The traditional A–F grading scale has thirteen levels of performance. If there are not explainable distinctions between a B+ and a B, and a C+ and a B–, then thirteen levels is too many—and when are there ever 101 discrete levels of achievement? Having numerous levels or impressive calculations does not make an assessment more "objective"; in fact, misleadingly precise results have the opposite effect. This happens so often in education that we have stopped noticing it. Although the examples in this book do not include it for space, having an "insufficient information" level avoids forcing an evaluator to make an uninformed (and usually negative) judgment. Basing evaluations on progress toward learning goals, rather than on grading conventions, is a crucial step toward fair and accurate assessment.

FEEDBACK

Feedback happens when the assessor communicates information from an assessment to a student. The process of gathering and evaluating information, providing feedback, and reassessing is called the **feedback loop**, represented by figure 4.1—a concept familiar to anyone who has observed a private lesson or rehearsal. The feedback loop, the assessment steps in figure 1.1, and the assessment cycle in figure 3.1 are all variations of the same concept.

Research has shown quality feedback to have a sizeable positive effect on student performance.[2] However, not all feedback is equally educative. Feedback can be classified as either evaluative or descriptive. **Evaluative feedback** is a judgment, an appraisal of quality. **Quantitative feedback**

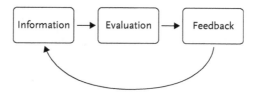

Figure 4.1: Feedback loop

is evaluative feedback given as numbers, grades, or percentages. In contrast, **descriptive feedback** helps the student answer the AfL questions ("Where am I going?" "Where am I now?" "How do I get there?"). Descriptive feedback leads to improvement more directly than evaluative feedback. Some students, particularly struggling students, do not have the tools to know "how to get there" or even "where they are" from evaluative feedback. Students given favorable evaluative feedback with no Next Steps may assume that no further action is necessary, and students given negative evaluative feedback with no Next Steps may feel as though success is unattainable. Evaluative feedback has a role—a supporting role—in summative assessment. During formative assessment, even including quantitative feedback alongside descriptive feedback may inhibit student learning. The best approach is often to avoid numbers and judgments altogether.

Music teachers sometimes have a habit of giving feedback that does not specify how to improve (e.g., "Listen!" "Check the key signature!" "Keep practicing that!"). If students already knew how to fix their problems, they would probably have done it already! Many music teachers provide descriptive feedback that tells students "where they are going," such as:

"This section is marked legato."

However, the feedback should also tell the students where they are:

"This section is marked legato. Right now you are playing staccato."

Effective feedback will also provide details about what to improve, and how:

"This section is marked legato. Right now you are playing staccato. Air that stops between notes makes it staccato. Make sure that you blow one continuous air stream from the A to the F♯."

Some teachers believe that evaluative feedback should be sufficient, that it is up to the students to determine Next Steps for themselves. While "spoon-feeding" certainly does not foster musical independence, neither does a strategy of deliberately withholding support from students who need it. Examples 3.1 and 3.2 are possibilities for scaffolding to help students with the self-evaluation process until they are experienced enough to do it alone. In my experience, more teachers provide too few Next Steps than too many.

When feedback is offered can be just as important as what feedback is offered. Students need actionable Next Steps, but they rarely retain feedback about steps far in the future. Teachers who press for results that are outside of students' ZPDs are risking alienation and lowered self-efficacy. The value in the feedback loop is in multiple cycles, as students' ZPDs expand slightly each time. Feedback is only effective if it is willingly and accurately processed by students. As Dylan Wiliam writes, "We need to start from where the learner *is*, not where we would like the learner to be."[3] If a student is flustered or defensive, he or she might be better able to receive important information a different day. Personal praise or criticism is an invitation to performance goals and fixed mindsets.

Feedback should be phrased affirmatively. "Don't breathe there" does not show the student how to hit the target; "Keep building the *crescendo* until . . ." does. "Don'ts" don't provide Next Steps for improvement. Feedback is ultimately about how to do better next time. Maybe we should call it "feedforward" instead.

EVALUATION AND FEEDBACK METHODS

Evaluations may be designed according to different **criteria**, or facets of the learning or task—like the categories on a traditional judge's sheet. ("Dimensions" are synonymous with criteria.) As elaborated in Chapter 2, precise criteria are essential for effective evaluation. AfL emphasizes criteria derived from learning targets (skills and understandings) rather than the task itself (such as neatness).

Introduced in the previous section, levels are used to describe the degrees of achievement. Discriminating between levels is relatively unimportant in formative assessment; descriptive feedback is most important. However, distinguishing between levels is a central goal of summative assessment. **Descriptors** are titles for the performance levels, such as "proficient" or "needs improvement." Educative descriptors use criterion referencing, such as "meets standards," rather than norm referencing, such as "outstanding" or "below average." Descriptors should also use nonjudgmental language. It is easy for students to apply terms like "superior" or "poor" to themselves rather than a work sample. This may lead to a fixed mindset instead of a focus on how to improve. Table 4.1 contains common descriptors. Humorous or otherwise student-centered descriptors are also effective and can keep assessment engaging.

Table 4.1: RUBRIC DESCRIPTORS

	Top-level descriptors	Middle-level descriptors	Bottom-level descriptors
Recommended	• Proficient • Fluent • Consistent • Complete • Strong	• Developing • Inconsistent • On the way • Almost there • Approaching	• Novice • Beginning • Emerging • Keep working • Not yet
Not recommended	• Outstanding • Superior • No mistakes	• Average • Fair • Some issues	• Below average • Poor • Inadequate

Evaluation of closed-ended items

Typically, closed-ended items have a single correct answer. If distractors are chosen strategically, then all incorrect answers have associated feedback. This feedback can be communicated to students in several ways. If the assessment only uses the left side of the page, then teachers can create a "feedback page" on the right side. The feedback page can be photocopied onto each student's assessment after the assessments are completed (as in Example 4.1). Technology allows teachers to create selected response assessments that provide immediate feedback, often providing individual and class performance reports for each item (see Chapter 10).

Organizing results by topic enables students and teachers to quickly arrive at Next Steps and streamlines reteaching and retesting by isolating the area or areas in which follow-up is needed. **Subscores** are student scores broken down by topic or learning target. Subscores are nearly always more useful than total scores. Indeed, subscores eliminate the need for a

Example 4.1: Feedback column copied onto student assessment

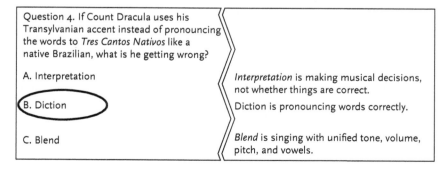

Example 4.2: Closed-ended assessment with subscores

English & Italian meanings
Your score: ___ / 5

1. What does the word dynamics mean?_____

_____

2. What does mezzo forte mean in English? _____
3. What does piano mean in English? _____
4. How do musicians write "very loud" in Italian? _____
5. How do musicians write "soft" in Italian? _____

Louder or softer?
Your score: ___ / 5

1. Which is louder, forte or fortissimo? _____
2. Which is softer, mezzo forte or fortissimo? _____
3. Which is softer, mezzo forte or mezzo piano? _____
4. Which is louder, piano or pianissimo? _____
5. Which is softer, piano or mezzo piano? _____

---

total. Teachers can easily provide subscores by organizing the questions by topic or skill (Example 4.2). Software allows the teacher to randomize the questions if desired, but "tag" each question with a learning target to provide subscore reports.

Checklists

Checklists of success criteria are a straightforward way to evaluate whether student work met one or more criteria. They may not seem ideal for nuanced appraisal, but they can combine efficiency and insight when carefully designed (Example 4.3). This method of using checklists tells the student where she is going and where she is now but does not provide information about how to get there. In order to embed feedback for improvement, checklists can be written as Next Steps instead, as in Example 4.4.

Rating scales

A **rating scale** is a simple performance progression. A teacher could assign a single overall score such as 1 to 4 or have multiple rating scales for different criteria (Example 4.5). It is difficult to embed descriptive feedback into a rating scale, since what each level means is not specified.

Example 4.3: Checklist

□ The crescendo got noticeably louder

□ The crescendo was gradual

□ The pitch stayed the same during the crescendo

□ The tone quality was good during the crescendo

□ The decrescendo got noticeably softer

□ The decrescendo was gradual

□ The pitch stayed the same during the decrescendo

□ The tone quality was good during the decrescendo

Example 4.4: Checklist written as Next Steps

Next time you play a crescendo:

□ Make sure you start <u>soft</u> and get <u>loud</u>

□ Make sure that the volume changes gradually rather than all at once

□ Listen to make sure you keep your pitch the same, and especially make sure you don't accidentally go sharp

□ To make sure your tone stays good during a crescendo, keep your embouchure relaxed and don't get <u>too</u> loud

□ Remember that soft playing still requires a big breath

□ Keep doing what you are doing!

Next time you play a decrescendo:

□ Make sure you start <u>loud</u> and get <u>soft</u>

□ Make sure that the volume changes gradually rather than all at once

□ Listen to make sure you keep your pitch the same, and especially make sure you don't accidentally go flat

□ Remember that soft playing still requires a big breath

□ Keep doing what you are doing!

Other comments:

Example 4.5: Rating scale

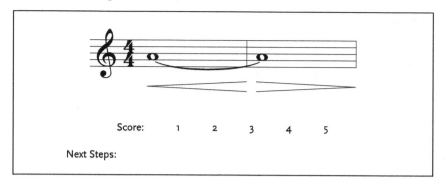

Score: 1   2   3   4   5

Next Steps:

Example 4.6: Rating scale with descriptors

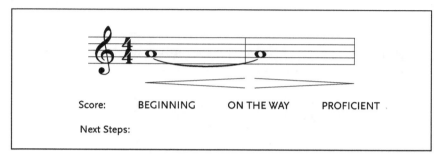

Score: BEGINNING   ON THE WAY   PROFICIENT

Next Steps:

Rating scales may also use level descriptors, as in Example 4.6. Descriptors can make the meaning of each level more clear to students and teachers, although there is still uncertainty about, for example, the difference between "on the way" and "proficient."

An issue with rating scales in music education is that tasks and concepts are frequently multifaceted. In these instances, an overall score does not inform the student about which facets were strong and which still need attention. The solution is to use a separate rating scale for each criterion, analogous to subscores (Example 4.7). Many festival judge sheets are multiple rating scales.

Rating scales using both descriptors and multiple criteria can be even more informative, as in Example 4.8. Still, there is no explicit information about why student work would belong in a given level.

Rubrics

A **rubric** is a scoring guide. Rubrics are similar to rating scales. In addition to lists of success criteria (sometimes called "traits") and levels, rubrics have **indicators**, which are specific descriptions associated with each

Example 4.7: Rating scale with multiple criteria

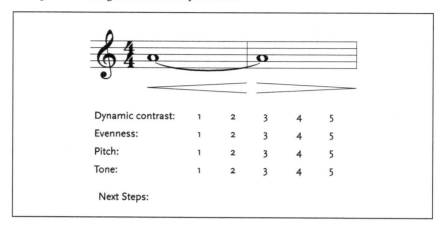

Dynamic contrast:	1	2	3	4	5
Evenness:	1	2	3	4	5
Pitch:	1	2	3	4	5
Tone:	1	2	3	4	5

Next Steps:

Example 4.8: Rating scale with multiple criteria and descriptors

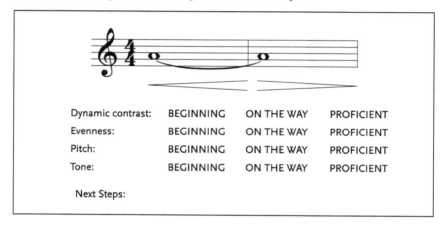

Dynamic contrast:	BEGINNING	ON THE WAY	PROFICIENT
Evenness:	BEGINNING	ON THE WAY	PROFICIENT
Pitch:	BEGINNING	ON THE WAY	PROFICIENT
Tone:	BEGINNING	ON THE WAY	PROFICIENT

Next Steps:

level of performance. For example, the indicator for Level 1 might be "The rhythms were barely recognizable," while Level 3 might be "The rhythms were all or nearly all correct." Because levels of performance are clearly defined, rubrics are more reliable (i.e., consistent and fair) than rating scales. (Still, the word "objective" should be used with caution.) Rubrics take more time to develop than rating scales, but the clarity that the teacher achieves by carefully considering criteria and indicators often leads to more precise instruction and assessment.

Rubrics that combine all indicators into a single global criterion are called **holistic rubrics**. In contrast, **Analytic rubrics** have multiple criteria, with separate indicators for each. Analytic and holistic rubrics each shine in certain situations. Teachers may find holistic rubrics to be more effective for summative assessment, situations in which they know

Example 4.9: Holistic rubric

Level 3	Level 2	Level 1
Clear dynamic contrast, smooth dynamic changes, and consistent tone and pitch. **Next steps:**	Dynamic contrast was small but noticeable; there may be minor issues with smoothness, consistent tone, and/or consistent pitch. **Next steps:**	There was no difference in the dynamics, or smoothness, consistent tone, and/or consistent pitch hindered the performance. **Next steps:**

Example 4.10: Analytic rubric

	Level 3	Level 2	Level 1
Dynamic contrast	It was easy to hear a difference in dynamics for both the crescendo <u>and</u> the diminuendo	It was easy to hear a difference in dynamics for the crescendo <u>or</u> the diminuendo, or there was only a moderate difference in dynamics.	There was hardly any difference in the dynamics.
Evenness	The dynamic changes happened smoothly <u>and</u> evenly for both the crescendo <u>and</u> the diminuendo.	The dynamic change happened smoothly and evenly for the crescendo <u>or</u> the diminuendo, but was sudden or uneven on the other.	The dynamic changes were not smooth or even. They may have been sudden, or out of control.
Pitch	The pitch stayed consistent during both the crescendo <u>and</u> the decrescendo.	The pitch stayed consistent during the crescendo <u>or</u> the decrescendo, but went noticeably sharp or flat on the other.	The pitch went noticeably sharp or flat on both the crescendo and the decrescendo.
Tone	Tone quality was consistent the whole time.	Tone quality was mostly consistent, only changing when it was very loud or very soft.	Tone quality suffered when the note got loud and when it got soft.

Next Steps:

- Focus on transferable learning targets rather than task specifics.
- Use consistent and student-friendly language.
- Use affirmative language for indicators (e.g., "correct notes" instead of "no wrong notes").
- Use encouraging indicators for lower levels.
- Use the leftmost column for the highest level to show students "where they are going"; show students only the leftmost column when introducing the assignment.
- Use rubric language during instruction and rehearsals.
- Design rubrics or rubric sections applicable across many assessments.
- Involve students in the creation of rubrics by evaluating anonymous exemplars.

they will provide narrative feedback or checkbox comments alongside the rubric, or evaluations of straightforward tasks. Analytic rubrics are at their best in formative assessment when they prompt descriptive feedback and "show students the target," particularly with complex tasks—especially when they use student-friendly language. Analytic rubrics do not address "the glue that holds a piece of work together,"[4] but this may not be the focus early in the learning process.

Rubrics are also effective for situations where teachers have traditionally used percentages derived from counting correct and incorrect responses. Suppose string students are playing the A Major scale. If the teacher merely counts correct and incorrect notes, a student could forget the G♯ both times and receive a 13 out of 15, or 87 percent—an unfortunate result considering that the student has not grasped the central note in A Major. A rubric such as Example 4.11 helps teacher and student focus on the most important elements of a task. The same approach is effective for written work. If questions on closed-ended assessments (e.g., written tests) are grouped by learning target, then rubrics can provide a more valid representation of student accomplishment than a percentage. Example 4.12 could be used for the quiz in Example 4.2.

Comments

Comments are verbal or written descriptive feedback. Individual narrative comments are the only way to do justice to certain types of student work.

Example 4.11: Scale test rubric

Got it!	Almost!	Not yet!
All notes were correct. **Next Steps:**	The notes were correct either ascending or descending, but not both. **Your notes to watch are:**	You need more practice with the notes in this key signature. **Your notes to watch are:**

Example 4.12: Rubric for closed-ended assessments

	Got it!	Almost!	Not yet!
English & Italian Meanings	You have a solid understanding of this concept. **Next Steps:**	You are well on your way to understanding this concept. **Remember that:**	You are not yet demonstrating an understanding of this concept. **Remember that:**
Louder or softer?	You have a solid understanding of this concept. **Next Steps:**	You are well on your way to understanding this concept. **Remember that:**	You are not yet demonstrating an understanding of this concept. **Remember that:**

When student work is personal, creative, or emotionally involved, a rating scale or off-the-shelf comment may feel inadequate or dismissive. Narrative comments are uniquely effective for nuanced conversation, probing questions, and personal validation, which are important but neglected facets of educational communication. The flexibility of narrative comments is their strength, but they also require thoughtfulness on the part of the teacher. Comments are often used in conjunction with other evaluation methods to address individual learners' needs in ways that checkboxes or rubrics cannot. Beginning comments with a student's name can emphasize the personal nature of the relationship between teacher and student. Without the name, comments can feel abrupt or cold.

Teachers often find themselves writing the same comments over and over. Particularly for straightforward tasks, assessments can include checkboxes with common feedback. Example 4.13 is the rubric in example 4.10 combined with the checklist from Example 4.4. This approach enables teachers to give descriptive feedback and Next Steps to a large number of

Example 4.13: Rubric with checkbox comments

	Level 3	Level 2	Level 1
Dynamic contrast	It was easy to hear a difference in dynamics for both the crescendo <u>and</u> the diminuendo	It was easy to hear a difference in dynamics for the crescendo <u>or</u> the diminuendo, or there was only a moderate difference in dynamics.	There was hardly any difference in the dynamics.
Evenness	The dynamic changes happened smoothly <u>and</u> evenly for both the crescendo <u>and</u> the diminuendo.	The dynamic change happened smoothly and evenly for the crescendo <u>or</u> the diminuendo, but was sudden or uneven on the other.	The dynamic changes were not smooth or even. They may have been sudden, or out of control.
Pitch	The pitch stayed consistent during both the crescendo <u>and</u> the decrescendo.	The pitch stayed consistent during the crescendo <u>or</u> the decrescendo, but went noticeably sharp or flat on the other.	The pitch went noticeably sharp or flat on both the crescendo and the decrescendo.
Tone	Tone quality was consistent the whole time.	Tone quality was mostly consistent, only changing when it was very loud or very soft.	Tone quality suffered when the note got loud and when it got soft.

Next Steps for the <u>crescendo</u>:

□ Make sure you start <u>soft</u> and get <u>loud</u>

□ Make sure that the volume changes gradually rather than all at once

□ Listen to make sure you keep your pitch the same, and especially make sure you don't accidentally go sharp

□ Remember that soft playing still requires a big breath and lots of air

Next Steps for the <u>decrescendo</u>:

□ Make sure you start <u>loud</u> and get <u>soft</u>

□ Make sure that the volume changes gradually rather than all at once

□ Listen to make sure you keep your pitch the same, and especially make sure you don't accidentally go flat

□ Remember that soft playing still requires a big breath and lots of air

Other Next Steps:

students efficiently. While it would be desirable for every student to receive individualized narrative feedback, for many teachers quickly giving descriptive feedback to many students is a better choice than not doing individual assessment at all due to time constraints. When the situation warrants it, narrative comments can supplement or replace the pre-written ones. However, there are many cases when the range of likely feedback is limited and predictable. The more closed-ended the task, the more appropriate checkbox comments and rubrics will be.

For self and peer assessment, comments can be structured using "sentence starters." Many teachers are familiar with protocols such as "plus/minus," which is one positive comment and one constructive comment, but there are countless others. If students are already using a schoolwide peer feedback system, it will probably transfer to music painlessly. Other possibilities include:

- Something to keep doing . . . Something to think about . . .
- I notice . . . I value . . . I wonder . . .
- ABC: Agree with . . . Build upon . . . Challenge . . .
- Thank you for . . . Your next steps might involve . . .

Teachers should monitor written and verbal comments closely. Judgmental statements and unclear or misleading advice hinder learning and camaraderie. It is frequently wise to give students *almost* all of their peers' feedback forms. If peer feedback is collected electronically, the teacher may find it advantageous to rewrite some comments, preserving the useful aspects of a critique while removing harsh or otherwise unhelpful elements.

CONSIDERATIONS FOR EVALUATION

To rubric or not to rubric

Analytic rubrics and rating scales work best for performance tasks that lend themselves to deconstruction into criteria and levels. Of course, not every situation works this way. Rubrics cannot capture every facet of student performance. As noted in chapter 1, there is a concern that reductionist student evaluation—sometimes called **rubricizing**—discourages students' curiosity and divergent thinking by identifying a single end goal and a single path toward it. Still, rubrics are effective when the learning objectives and performance tasks have fewer divergent possibilities. For example, the skill of performing a crescendo and decrescendo is not a natural opportunity for students to demonstrate divergent thinking. When their use would not stifle student innovation, rubrics' ability to facilitate Assessment for Learning is a compelling reason to develop and use them.

When reductionism is a concern, a holistic rubric accompanied by verbal or written narrative comments might be more appropriate.

Determining criteria

It is never possible to include all potentially relevant criteria in advance; teachers decide which criteria are most important for evaluation. Each criterion may be more or less relevant in different situations, and the need to consider them all may inhibit the assessor's ability to focus on the most salient aspects of a performance.[5] All teachers have had the frustration of trying to fit a square evaluation peg into a round evaluation-tool hole. (Are we *really* likely to be equally concerned with rhythmic accuracy, blend, and expression in Lauridsen's *O Magnum Mysterium*, Barber's *Adagio for Strings*, and Ives's *Country Band March*?) However, assessment tools can be designed to be flexible, as in Example 4.14. The use of **emergent criteria**—waiting to see which elements of a task are most relevant in each situation—can help to address the issue of reductionism. Criteria in traditional analytic rubrics or rating scales (like judge sheets) can be made emergent by the simple addition of the phrase "where applicable."[6] Students and teachers

Example 4.14: Evaluation with emergent criteria

Overall Evaluation
□ Great performance!   □ Some good things!   □ This hasn't come together yet!

Evaluator: select up to three Hot Topics that were the biggest reasons for your overall evaluation. Possible Hot Topics include preparation, tone, tempo, musical expression, note accuracy, rhythm accuracy, dynamic contrast, musical style, technique, balance, blend, tuning, confidence, body language, and anything else that was relevant to this performance.

Hot Topic #1 was: _____	□ This helped your performance today. □ This hindered your performance today.	Comments:
Hot Topic #2 was: _____	□ This helped your performance today. □ This hindered your performance today.	Comments:
Hot Topic #3 was: _____	□ This helped your performance today. □ This hindered your performance today.	Comments:
Next Steps and other comments:		

can also collaborate to determine individualized evaluation criteria for non-traditional or creative endeavors.[7] One reason that teachers have not traditionally used flexible criteria is the issue of uniform scoring by addition, which is addressed next.

To total or not to total

The "__ out of __" scoring paradigm is entrenched in schools. However, total scores are often unhelpful for communication about learning. Students do not need a total score to see how to improve; in fact, the total can inhibit their ability to receive improvement-focused feedback. In addition, the total score often fails to be logical or educative. Stating that, for example, "notes plus rhythms plus technique plus expression equals music" does not align with most music educators' views on artistry.[8] As formative assessments are best left out of the gradebook (see Chapter 8), the total score can usually be abandoned. If an overall score is desired for summative assessment, placing it at the top emphasizes that the musical elements that follow are only relevant insofar as they contribute to the artistic product. This is how many people intuitively evaluate. We first ask ourselves "How good was that?" and only ask "Why?" afterward.[9] Assessment can be designed to work the same way.

Assessment in the spiral curriculum

Ensemble classes typically feature a spiral curriculum where skills like tone and concepts like interpretation are revisited in cycles. Teachers often champion the notion that there is always room to grow, even if a student has met the standard for a particular experience level or is the most accomplished performer in the room. Misuse of the "clear targets" approach can undermine this pursuit of continuous improvement. Teachers can include Next Steps for even the top levels of rubrics to encourage continuous improvement, and they can differentiate curricula so that, for example, rather than everyone being assigned the same two scales, each student is assigned to learn their own next two scales.

Music teachers often say that they would like assessment to differentiate between students who are meeting expectations and those whose performance is exceptional. This is rarely necessary. An exceptional student who receives a top rating of "proficient" is unlikely to feel slighted, and most exceptional musicians are not primarily motivated by classroom assessment in any case. Still, the desire to show that there is room for improvement is understandable. Including a top-level descriptor such as "exemplary" or "distinguished" can accomplish this provided that this level receives the same grade as the one below it. There must also be clearly stated criteria for what makes a performance "distinguished" in the interest of fairness.[10] Caution is warranted, however. Many students and families are unsettled by anything other than the best possible score, no matter how often the teacher reminds them that it does not represent failure or a deduction. Grade inflation can result, rendering the distinction between "proficient" and "exemplary" meaningless.

When there are students of varying experience in the same ensemble, assessment can advance the idea that standards are higher for students with more experience. They can also design the top achievement level to mean different things to different students. For example, "meets standards" for instrument tuning could be Level 3 for freshmen, Level 4 for sophomores, and so on, or Level 3 for students in Concert Orchestra, Level 4 in Philharmonic, and Level 5 in Symphony.

Targeted assessment

Focusing assessments on one or very few learning targets at a time enables teachers to give the most relevant feedback and students to process and apply it more easily. Consider the A Major scale example in Example 4.12, where the evaluation was potentially diluted by equally considering the A and E (which the student is unlikely to forget) and the C♯ and the G♯ (the crucial notes). This evaluation would be further diluted by including instrument position, bow hold, and rhythms. In addition, if teachers (or students engaged in self or peer evaluation) are attempting to focus on too many things, they are truly focusing on none. While targeted assessment works well for discrete musical elements, it requires planning to ensure comprehensiveness. Teachers must also account for the risk of being reductionist by overly compartmentalizing musical elements.

Integrated assessment

Chapter 1 introduced the idea that musical elements do not function separately from one another. For example, an ensemble's tempo problems may be related to articulation. In such an instance, the solution to tempo problems is to address articulation, which doesn't quite fit into a "tempo" criterion.

Example 4.15: Integrated ensemble blend rubric

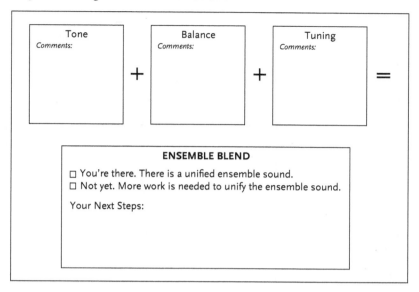

Such a scenario could be reported through emergent criteria or open-ended or checkbox comments. However, assessments can also be designed to explicitly represent connections between individual musical skills and understandings and the reasons behind those skills and understandings. Traditional judge-sheet evaluation does not account for this; all musical elements are portrayed as equally important in all situations. Once an assessor decides to use "overall" scores rather than "total" scores, the need for an inflexible scoresheet fades, and alternatives (e.g., Examples 4.15 and 4.16) come to light.

Formative and summative assessment revisited

Most of the examples in this book are designed to be used formatively. They feature analytic rather than holistic approaches, concerned with elicitation of improvement-focused feedback rather than classifying or ranking students. However, summative assessment is usually necessary as a basis for school-mandated grades. While breaking complex tasks into component parts is crucial in formative assessment, summative assessment ideally involves synthesis: the purest representation of standards or objectives. Even though the authentic tasks described in Chapter 3 are ideal vehicles for summative assessment, music teachers do not always ask students to engage with music independently in those ways. No matter

Example 4.16: Integrated performance evaluation

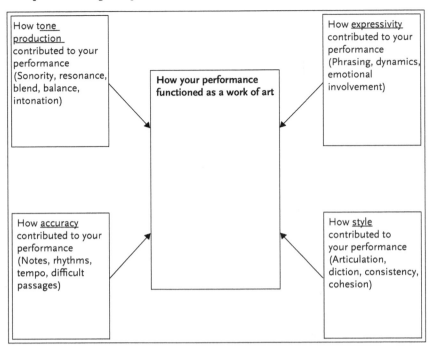

| How <u>tone production</u> contributed to your performance (Sonority, resonance, blend, balance, intonation) | **How your performance functioned as a work of art** | How <u>expressivity</u> contributed to your performance (Phrasing, dynamics, emotional involvement) |

| How <u>accuracy</u> contributed to your performance (Notes, rhythms, tempo, difficult passages) | | How <u>style</u> contributed to your performance (Articulation, diction, consistency, cohesion) |

which method is used, summative assessment usually involves a number of different learning targets. This intensifies the need for holistic evaluation and emergent criteria. Examples 4.14 and 4.12 would function well as summative assessment, while Example 4.10 or totals and percentages might not. Students deserve in-class practice and formative assessment prior to all summative tasks; this is an opportunity for formative use of the summative evaluation. Different tasks demonstrate different skills and understandings. Planning is crucial to ensure that summative assessment and resulting grades reflect the teacher's vision for students.

DATA-DRIVEN INSTRUCTION

Data-driven instruction has become an infamous educational buzzword. As with any ubiquitous phrase, it has come to mean different things to different people. Using information about students to make better educational decisions should be uncontroversial—that is the premise of this book. Unfortunately, data-driven instruction has many teachers frustrated. To reprise Alfie Kohn, sometimes an overzealous teacher or administrator misses the forest while counting the trees and insists on seemingly purposeless or endless data collection, or uses data to justify illogical decisions.

Still, few would argue that data has no role in education. Instead of the term "data-driven," which seems to emphasize data over the expertise of educators, the term **data-informed** might be preferable.[11] Data is only suitable for "driving" decisions on the rare occasion when it represents a comprehensive view of an issue. Nevertheless, examination of data can uncover important truths about who is enrolled in music classes, what they are doing, and how they are doing. What if there are thirty-five boys in sixth grade orchestra but only eleven by eighth grade? How many students used that carefully crafted Practice Guide at least twice, and do they have higher memorization scores?

Three types of data (Table 4.2) may be the most relevant to music educators hoping to make decisions about their instruction or program structure. **Input data** is background information about students that might be associated with their progress. **Process data** is information about how students work and learn. **Output data** deals with student achievement or progress. Dylan Wiliam and Siobhán Leahy further advocated for "decision-driven data collection,"[12] in which educators first determine the educational decisions or questions at hand and then collect data accordingly. Data use without a clear purpose can feel productive but lack tangible benefits. Data used by teachers to decide not which students to help but to presuppose which students "probably won't succeed anyway" is unethical.

Table 4.2: TYPES OF DATA

Input data	Process data	Output data
• Voice part or instrument	• Amount and quality of practice	• Any assessment results
• Grade level	• Use of class time	• Enrollment or
• Years of experience in school music	• Use of warm-up or preparation time	retention
• Gender, race, or ethnicity	• Use of pencil for markings	• Extracurricular participation
• Sending school	• Completion of class work or review packets	• Honors or awards
• English-language learning	• Attendance at practice or review sessions	• Acceptance to selective ensembles
• Exceptionality or disability		
• Reading scores	• Voice care	
• Attendance or discipline history	• Instrument, bow, or reed quality or maintenance	
• Poverty	• Private lessons	
• How students get to school		

Teachers might be interested in input data to learn who might need support in a particular area. For example, suppose a choir teacher looking at the results of a text-memorization assessment sees that English-language learners have lower scores on average. In the future, the teacher can support those students from the beginning of the memorization process, possibly in consultation with an ELL specialist. Similarly, students from a particular sending school may practice less often because the school is further away and they struggle with instruments on the bus. A teacher may relate process data about how students approach sight-singing to output data about their performance, using the results to improve instruction in the future.

Simple examination of output data is also often revelatory. Aggregate class performance often has obvious trends. In fact, most teachers have informally used data in this way without calling it "data use," for example by noticing that beginners tend to struggle with dotted quarter notes year after year. **Disaggregated** class performance, or data broken down by groups of students, can be even more eye-opening. Process and output data that are disaggregated by input data have the potential to improve instruction and also teacher advocacy. For example, choir teachers frequently bristle when new students are dropped into their advanced groups midyear. Data can be a compelling part of the case for ending this practice.

Music teachers looking to begin using data in their classrooms can select a single type of input or output data that is related to existing classroom goals. Output data such as the types of rhythms, intervals, or pieces that students tend to do more or less successfully are often easy for teachers to identify, particularly if assessment results can be compared across classes or years. For all their flaws, electronic gradebooks can facilitate this process, especially when subscores are recorded over time. The next step is to determine why a particular trend is happening and what the logical implications are. Might some students be struggling with key enabling skills? If so, are data available on the enabling skills? A teacher who frequently uses individual assessment strategies is already on her way to productively using data in her instruction. "Data" doesn't have to be a dirty word.

SUMMARY

After assessment information has been collected, it requires interpretation and action. Nonjudgmental feedback phrased in words and containing

Next Steps for improvement supports learning more than cold-sounding numbers. There are many methods for evaluating student work. Effective evaluation tools are selected on the basis of coherence with the student task and the learning it is intended to evoke. All evaluation methods are better in some situations than others. Even though many teachers are conditioned to see "data" as pernicious, data can be a powerful tool to guide instruction.

TERMS

- Criterion-referenced
- Norm-referenced
- Construct-referenced
- Levels
- Reliable
- Feedback
- Feedback loop
- Evaluative feedback
- Quantitative feedback
- Descriptive feedback
- Criteria
- Descriptors
- Subscore
- Checklist
- Rating scale
- Rubric
- Indicators
- Holistic rubric
- Analytic rubric
- Comments
- Rubricizing
- Emergent criteria
- Data-driven instruction
- Data-informed instruction
- Input data
- Process data
- Output data
- Disaggregated

ACTIVITIES

4.1. List the evaluation methods from this chapter that might best correspond with each of the assessment methods in Chapter 3. Also compile a list of any potential pairings that seem like egregious mismatches.

4.2. Choose any performance task. List the enabling skills, and use them to develop a rating scale (or multiple rating scales if appropriate), a holistic rubric, and an analytic rubric. Make a list of descriptive feedback items (including Next Steps) you would be likely to give. Include these as checkboxes on your assessments. Reflect on your process. What did you realize about the task or concept as part of creating your assessment?

4.3. Develop your own integrated assessment in the style of Example 4.15 or 4.16. Choose a skill or a facet of a skill. List the components. How do they work together to comprise the skill you chose?

4.4. Make a list of "I wonder if . . ." questions that looking at input, process, or outcome data might help to answer. If you knew the answers to your questions, what would you do as the teacher?

4.5. Make an audio or video recording of your teaching. Examine the verbal feedback you give during the lesson on the recording. Does it tend to be more evaluative or more descriptive? Does it include Next Steps? Is it followed with reassessment, to make sure the student(s) were able to implement it?

4.6. Summarize the differences between a total score and an overall score. When might each be useful?

SECTION TWO
Applications

CHAPTER 5
Musical Understandings

The ultimate responsibility of a teacher or conductor lies in developing the abilities of the student or performer, allowing errors and mistakes in the road of growth, and providing the breadth of experience that will allow the individual student to reach their potential.

Donald Hunsberger[1]

Box 5.1: CHAPTER 5 ESSENTIAL QUESTIONS

1. What is the difference between off-the-podium and on-the-podium instruction?
2. In what ways can assessment help students improve their musical abilities?

TEACH PIECES, OR TEACH MUSIC?

When asked to picture an ensemble music teacher, most people—including most music teachers—would probably describe the discourses of the professional conductor: podiums, batons, and inspiration. While a conductor on a podium is certainly the traditional model, it is far from the only paradigm in which music learning can occur. In most instances, instruction **on the podium** has concert preparation at its core; individual knowledge and abilities are improved during the course of preparing for the performance. In contrast, instruction **off the podium** is a setting more reminiscent of a traditional classroom in which the primary goal is improvement in students' fundamental knowledge and abilities. Off-the-podium instruction is teaching for **transfer**—the ability to apply previously learned material in new situations.[2] The premise is that students with stronger musical abilities will transfer those abilities to each performance.

These approaches are not mutually exclusive, but rather complementary. The majority of music teachers seek to balance the twin goals of performing and understanding. The question is not whether individuals' musical abilities are improved by learning performance repertoire, or whether performances are improved by building individual abilities. Both statements are true; the question is a matter of proportion. To be sure, some outstanding teachers manage to achieve understanding in a primarily rehearsal-driven environment. Nevertheless, many impressive ensembles are populated by students whose musical understandings are limited to the parts they have learned to perform. In many classrooms, shifting the balance toward individual abilities would be beneficial both for students' musical learning and the performance result. The proverb "If you give a man a fish, he'll eat for a day; if you teach him to fish, he'll eat for a lifetime" is relevant to decisions about whether to teach pieces or teach principles.

Ensemble teachers frequently assume that students have, or should have, accumulated a great deal of musical expertise. For them, just like the Maestro, rehearsing is largely a matter of applying these previously acquired abilities to new musical material. Unfortunately, a considerable amount of this kind of concert preparation turns out to be remediating deficits in fundamental skills or understandings that the students were presumed to have. If a singer generally has trouble singing in head voice, he or she will have trouble singing in head voice in the concert. If a cellist doesn't understand that accidentals carry through the measure, then the concert music likely has wrong notes. Ensembles full of better musicians are inherently better ensembles, during this concert and in the future. Sometimes teachers say that they "don't have time" for off-the-podium instruction or assessment. Even when efficiency is paramount, teachers don't have time *not* to know exactly which students can hold a harmony part, understand key signatures, remember the words, or play staccato!

CLASSROOM ASSESSMENT IN THE ENSEMBLE

On-the-podium instruction is best suited for performance preparation, while off-the-podium instruction is the most effective path to other targets. Teachers may wish to begin a concert cycle with more off-the-podium instruction and assessment of foundational abilities, gradually progressing to more on-the-podium synthesis as a concert nears. The teacher can more confidently ask students to apply their fundamental skills and understandings from the podium if assessment shows that students possess those abilities in the first place. This chapter will examine assessment strategies for Knowledge, Reasoning, Product, and Disposition targets. Skill targets comprise the next two chapters: fundamentals in Chapter 6, and performance preparation in Chapter 7. For ease of understanding, the examples in these chapters are intentionally straightforward. Teachers can apply the full variety of techniques from Chapters 3 and 4 when developing assessments for classroom use.

The examples in these chapters are similar to activities that music teachers may already use informally. Addressing these important concepts through formal assessment, often by having a written or electronic handout, is useful for all participants. Such a document does not have to look fancy and takes only minutes to create.

Assessment handouts that are created electronically have the twin advantages of being easy to revise and adapt for the future. Including student names, humorous examples, memes, celebrity pictures, and the like can promote student interest. Even if it feels cumbersome at first, creating

Table 5.1: ON AND OFF THE PODIUM

"On the podium" is naturally suited for:	"Off the podium" is naturally suited for:
• Informal assessment	• Formal or informal assessment
• Assessing the entire ensemble	• Assessing individuals
• Applying Knowledge, Reasoning, Skills, and Dispositions to concert repertoire	• Presenting new concepts
• Performance preparation assessment (PPA)	• Assessment of transferable fundamentals
• Anecdotal study of history, context, meaning, text	• In-depth study of history, context, meaning, text
• Class meetings as a concert draws near	• Class meetings early in a concert cycle

Box 5.2: REASONS TO USE A HANDOUT FOR CLASSROOM ASSESSMENT

- It clarifies the teacher's thinking about the exact steps to take.
- It reveals key enabling skills that should be included in the assessment.
- It helps students understand what they are supposed to be learning and what they are supposed to be doing.
- It requires all students to answer.
- It gives the teacher information about each student's progress because there is something to submit.
- It offers students the opportunity to practice necessary literacy skills.

digital or paper handouts can soon become second nature. Students can also record their thoughts on whiteboards or even verbalize them to classmates; the goal is to get everyone participating.

A simple self assessment such as Example 5.1 can help students "see" success and quickly appraise their own progress toward it. While Example 5.1 contains mainly Knowledge targets, the format is flexible enough to work with nearly any concept or skill. With this kind of self assessment, students are able to see their own progress and determine their own Next Steps—a core metacognitive strategy. Teachers could collect forms such as these as a diagnostic assessment and then do so again regularly throughout a unit as one component of ongoing formative assessment. Students could also keep the form in their folders and update it during a unit, possibly using a different shape around the numbers on successive occasions. Students who complete such a form using technology can provide real-time information to the teacher. Teachers often ask "Are there

Example 5.1: Progress monitoring self assessment

We're learning about tone quality. Where are you now?							
	Can you...	No way!					Oh yeah!
1.	Define "tone quality" in music?	o	1	2	3	4	5
2.	Describe why tone quality is important?	o	1	2	3	4	5
3.	Explain why we play warm-ups at the beginning of class?	o	1	2	3	4	5
4.	List some adjectives to describe good tone?	o	1	2	3	4	5
5.	List some adjectives to describe bad tone?	o	1	2	3	4	5
6.	Hear someone playing your instrument and evaluate the tone quality?	o	1	2	3	4	5
7.	Explain why breathing is important to tone quality for wind instruments?	o	1	2	3	4	5
8.	Explain why beating spots are important to tone quality for percussion players?	o	1	2	3	4	5
9.	Explain why equipment is important to both wind and percussion tone?	o	1	2	3	4	5
10.	List some strategies for making a good sound on *your* instrument?	o	1	2	3	4	5
11.	Play your instrument with good tone quality?	o	1	2	3	4	5
	My Next Steps:						

- Define
- Describe
- List
- Label

- Recognize
- Identify
- Explain

any questions?" but what if less-metacognitive students don't know that they *should* have questions?

KNOWLEDGE ASSESSMENT

On the surface, Knowledge seems straightforward to assess. However, students can recite facts without understanding them. For example, a student may be able to write a definition of legato on a worksheet but not know how it relates to staccato or marcato. The student may also categorize legato as a tempo marking; in her experience, legato always comes up with slow pieces. Similarities, differences, and categories may seem obvious to teachers who have been musicians for decades, but students often do not make connections on their own. The fact that musical terminology uses terms from different languages only compounds the issue.

One common way to help students organize their thinking is use of a **graphic organizer**, which provides students with a visual architecture that can help them make desired connections. Examples 5.2 through 5.9 are examples of malleable graphic organizers for Knowledge assessment. Example 5.10 is a playful take on graphic organizers designed to inspire music teachers' creativity with crafting their own assessments.

Box 5.4: WHAT KNOWLEDGE ASSESSMENTS MIGHT INCLUDE

1. The definition and/or English translation (*factual*)
2. Specific performance instructions (*procedural*)
3. How it relates to other musical concepts, or when this Knowledge should be used (*conceptual*)

Example 5.2: K-W-L ("Know–Want to know–Learned") no. 1

LEARNING TARGET: _I can define and order the 6 common dynamics_	
What I know mf=medium loud mp=medium soft f=loud p=soft	**What I want to know** Not sure about ff and pp
What I learned ff=very loud, pp=very soft pp, p, mp, mf, f, ff	**Questions I still have** We have way more violins than basses, so ... how do they all play the same dynamics? Isn't there fff too?

Example 5.3: K-W-L no. 2

Bow stroke	What I already know about it	Questions I have	What I learned
Detaché			
Martelé			
Legato			
Spiccato			

Example 5.4: Venn diagram

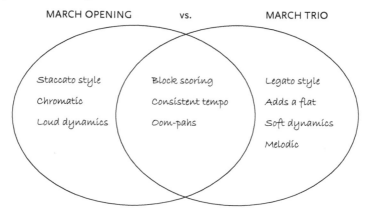

MARCH OPENING   vs.   MARCH TRIO

Staccato style   Block scoring   Legato style
Chromatic   Consistent tempo   Adds a flat
Loud dynamics   Oom-pahs   Soft dynamics
                                       Melodic

Example 5.5: More Venn diagram possibilities

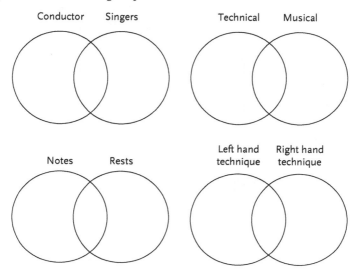

Conductor   Singers   Technical   Musical

Notes   Rests   Left hand   Right hand
                       technique   technique

Example 5.6: Frayer model

Definition in your own words	Facts or characteristics
Term:	
Examples	Non-examples

Example 5.7: Contrast and compare chart

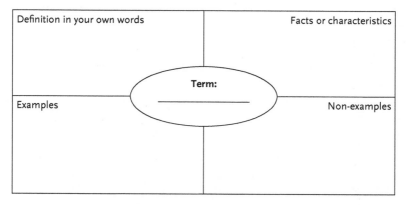

Snare drum		Timpani
	Pitched or non-pitched?	
	Heads on top, bottom, or both?	
	Wind instruments that often have similar parts	
	Types of sticks	
	Types of rolls	

Example 5.8: Knowledge table

Piece	Composer	Dates	Location	Reason or story	Other pieces	Fun fact
Bist du bei mir						
Sleep						
Walk in Jerusalem						

Example 5.9: Knowledge table no. 2

	What does this bow stroke mean in English?	How is this bow stroke notated in sheet music?	What would you say to help your stand partner play using this bow stroke?
Detaché			
Martelé			
Legato			
Spiccato			

Example 5.10: Terminology sorting

The apple doesn't fall too far from the orange tree! (Wait...???)

Word bank:

Piano	Presto	Adagio	Legato
Vivace	Staccato	Marcato	Pianissimo
Accent	Mezzo piano	Allegretto	Allegro
Diminuendo	Moderato	Andante	Tenuto
Mezzo forte	Fortissimo	Crescendo	Forte

Put the <u>dynamics</u> under the apple tree.

Put the <u>articulations</u> under the orange tree.

Put the <u>tempo markings</u> under the cherry tree.

BONUS: put the terms under each tree <u>in order</u>!

FOR NEXT TIME: make a list of any terms that were confusing, and write what they mean.

Example 5.11: Note-reading assessment

Accidentals Review: Tuba

1a. List the names of the three accidentals.
1b. Draw the symbol next to each one.

2. What's the point of accidentals?

3. How long do accidentals remain in effect?

4. Write the note names under each note. *Always use capital letters for note names.*

Music literacy foundations are nearly universal Knowledge in ensemble curricula. Note and rhythm assessments are commercially available, but they are straightforward to create and customize.

Selected response and written response are the most common approaches for Knowledge assessment. While graphic organizers are helpful, teachers should bear in mind that they are not the only ways to assess what students know. Simply asking students to write down the solfège syllables for the major scale or list the steps to tightening a bow provides valuable information for the teacher and student. Even if the assessment is not submitted, sharing in a peer group or using quick formative assessment techniques can quickly illuminate which students might need help. Example 5.12 is a procedural knowledge assessment that could be used in any of these ways. Whether the questions are asked is more important than how they are asked.

Example 5.12: Video analysis

Adapted from Timothy Fawkes

Listening for Tone and Expression

Today we are going to watch some videos of great orchestras and string players. Answer the questions for each piece.

1. Bass Concerto No. 2 (Bottesini), performed by Enrico Fagone

How would you describe the sound the soloist is making? Provide three descriptor words.

_____   _____   _____

2. Passacaglia (Handel), performed by Itzhak Perlman and Pinchas Zukerman

How would you describe the sound they are making at the beginning? Provide three descriptor words.

_____   _____   _____

Are Perlman and Zukerman using lots of bow or a little bow?_____

When the style changes, how is the sound different? Explain.

_____

_____

In this new section, are they using lots of bow or a little bow?_____

Why do you think they have made this choice? Explain.

_____

_____

3. String Quartet No. 8 (Shostakovich), performed by Mosaic Ensemble

How would you describe the sound they are making at the beginning? Provide three descriptor words.

_____   _____   _____

How is this sound different from the beginning of the Passacaglia? How are they using their bows to make it different? Explain.

_____

_____

Example 5.13: Tuning terms assessment

Tuning terms

What is the purpose of playing a tuning note at the beginning of a rehearsal or concert?

What can playing a tuning note *not* accomplish?

What tuning note(s) is/are most common for your instrument?

Why is this note (or are these notes) so common?

If your pitch is too *high*, then you are _____ .

You should adjust by _____ on your instrument.

If your pitch is too *low*, then you are _____ .

You should adjust by _____ on your instrument.

Where on your instrument do you make tuning adjustments?

What are 2 strategies you can use to hear yourself in the group during a tuning note?

1.

2.

What are "beats in the air?"

As "beats in the air" get faster, is it more in tune or more out of tune?

As "beats in the air" get slower, is it more in tune or more out of tune?

Example 5.14: Tonguing assessment

Tonguing Assessment: Brass

1. Why do we tongue notes when we play? _____

2. Where does your tongue touch your mouth when tonguing a note? _____

3. Which part of your tongue do you use for tonguing? _____

4. What word gets your tongue in the right place? _____

5. What 2 places should your tongue <u>not</u> touch?

    1.

    2.

6. When you tongue, should your lips stay apart, or should they close? _____

7. What should your lungs do when you tongue? _____

8. What are the 3 steps involved in tonguing a note?

    1.

    2.

    3.

9. How often do you think you tongue notes in band?

    ALWAYS   USUALLY   SOMETIMES   NEVER   NOT
SURE

Example 5.15: String shifting
Adapted from Timothy Fawkes

How would you explain shifting to a beginner?

How would you explain fingerboard positions to a beginner?

On the **A string**...

      1st position starts on the note _____.

      2nd position starts on the note _____.

      3rd position starts on the note _____.

      4th position starts on the note_____.

On the **D string**...

      1st position starts on the note _____.

      2nd position starts on the note _____.

      3rd position starts on the note _____.

      4th position starts on the note _____.

REASONING ASSESSMENT

Box 5.5: REASONING VERBS

- Summarize
- Analyze
- Problem-solve
- Predict
- Evaluate
- Compare
- Infer

The archetypal ensemble environment is one in which the performers execute what the Maestro dictates. However, one ensemble-friendly method of Reasoning assessment is engaging students in thought processes traditionally performed by the conductor. By providing them with the necessary supports and background knowledge, student input can play a role in large-group musical interpretation. In Examples 5.16 through 5.18, scaffolding

Example 5.16: Repertoire Analysis

Repertoire Analysis

Title of piece: _____

Is the piece from a larger work? If so, which one? _____

Who is the composer? _____

What do we know about the composer's life or career? _____
_____
_____

If there is an arranger, who is it? What do we know about the arranger? _____
_____

Are there any other pieces the composer has written that we might know? _____
_____

Does the title mean anything? If so, what? _____
_____

When, how, and/or why was the music written? _____
_____

What are we learning by learning to perform this piece? What seems to be our focus in
rehearsals? _____

Is there anything unusual or special about this piece?_____
_____

How does this piece relate to other pieces on this concert? _____
_____

Why I think my teacher picked this piece for us: _____
_____

What our audience might appreciate about this piece:_____
_____

What that means for me as a performer: _____
_____

Example 5.17: Interpretation guide

Part 1: Musical Structure Primer

1. What are the big sections of the music? Do any parts happen more than once?

2. How does the music start?

3. How does the music end?

4. Where is the music the loudest?

5. Where is it the softest?

6. If the piece has a key signature, are there any places where the composer changes keys or uses accidentals, especially a *lot* of accidentals?

7. List some places where the composer uses an idea (such as word, melody, rhythm, or instruments) in one way, and then repeats the same idea in a similar way:

8. Now, list some places where the composer uses an idea (word, melody, rhythm, instruments, etc.) in one way, and then changes something:

9. Where does your part do something interesting or unexpected?

10. What parts of the piece do you find most meaningful? Why?

Part 2: Interpretation guide

"Warm-up" question: define *interpretation* in music.

11. Look over your answers to questions 1–3 in the Musical Structure Primer. What answers did many of you have in common?

12. What answers were unique? If your group had any disagreements about answers, what were they?

13. Now, look at your answers to Questions 3–10. These are all clues to decisions we need to make for our interpretation of this music. Choose any answers that your group finds interesting, and then write how we can act upon that information when we perform this piece.

Measure(s)	What you noticed about the music	What we should emphasize in our performance

Example 5.18: Dynamic contrast planner

Dynamic contrast planner

Directions:

1. Write how you would explain "dynamic contrast" to someone who's never been in orchestra:

_____

_____

2. Write what you have to do as a player to achieve dynamic contrast: _____

_____

3. Write your dynamic marking for each part of the piece in the boxes below. If you don't play, get the dynamic marking from someone else—everyone has the same dynamics.

4. Listen and watch as we play the piece. Put an "X" in the box for each instrument family if members of that family are playing during those measures. What do you notice?

_____

_____

_____

Measure	Dynamic marking	Strings playing?	Woodwinds playing?	Brass playing?	Percussion playing?
1–4					
5–12					
13–20					
21–28					
29–32					
(etc.)					

5. Graph the dynamics along the line below. First, draw a dot for the group's dynamic marking at each measure. Next, draw lines to connect the dots. Finally, put a star above the place (or places) you think should be the loudest part of this section.

ff
f
mf
mp
p
pp

     1   5   9   13   17   21   25   29   33

6. List a few places where we should focus on achieving dynamic contrast:

_____

_____

_____

---

is provided for students who have little or no experience; a primer on relevant background knowledge is a seminal strategy for metacognition. Once students have demonstrated success with structured Reasoning tasks, they may need less guidance.

Some teachers wonder what would happen if the students are committed to a musical decision that goes against the teacher's best judgment. If this is a concern, the teacher could be intentional about which decisions will have student involvement or could establish the expectation that any decisions made by students can be re-evaluated after a period of time. After they live with an odd interpretation for a few days, students may come to the conclusion that it should be re-evaluated. This is an authentic part of the Reasoning process! The teacher can also provide varied reference recordings to provide an interpretive context. However, restrictions are often unnecessary. Students are simply unlikely to formulate and stand by nonsensical interpretations. Furthermore, unless a performance is formally adjudicated, audiences typically appreciate students' developing musical instincts—especially when students explain their process.

Evaluation and critique

Evaluation and critique are two types of Reasoning that are relevant to music classrooms. Thus, self and peer assessments can be Reasoning assessments themselves. Since learning targets are classified by the learning they are intended to evaluate, teachers hoping that a peer assessment will serve as Reasoning should judge students' work based on the quality of the evaluation itself, not the knowledge or skills that were the subject of the critique. Example 5.19 reflects such a focus. This approach has great potential for ensemble teachers wishing to incorporate a different kind of thinking into their classrooms. As described in Chapter 3, students often benefit from frequent and explicit reminders that their feedback is only helpful when it is music-focused and nonjudgmental.

Thought-provoking questions

Intriguing questions can also serve as the basis for Reasoning assessment. Students' critical thinking can be evaluated using a simple rubric or rating scale, such as Example 5.20. Knowledge is an enabling skill underlying all Reasoning assessments. To ensure that Reasoning is based on good information, teachers might use a "knowledge warm-up" at the beginning of

Example 5.19: Evaluation assessment

	BOOM!	Almost there!	Not yet! (Redo)
Using musical terms	You used relevant musical terminology that we learned in class, and used it correctly.	You used relevant and correct musical terminology some of the time, but not all of the time. **Remember that:**	Your description used little or no relevant or correct musical terminology. **Remember that:**
Listening, watching, and processing	You accurately perceived and described the performance.	Your listening and processing skills are developing. **Remember that:**	Your musical diagnoses did not accurately represent the performance. **Remember that:**
Giving feedback that is focused and respectful	Your feedback was on target, respectful, and supportive.	Your feedback skills are developing. **Remember that:**	For your feedback to be useful for peers, it needs to be respectful and focused. **Remember that:**
(Not graded) Your Next Steps with performance evaluation:	Your writing or speaking communicate your ideas clearly and professionally.	Your communication skills are developing. **Remember that:**	Communication skills are important! **Remember that:**

Your Next Steps with performance evaluation:

Example 5.20: Reasoning assessment

Were your ideas...			
...based on accurate information?	Success!	Getting there!	Getting started!
	Next Steps:		
...coherent and connected to the question at hand?	Success!	Getting there!	Getting started!
	Next Steps:		
...thoughtful, insightful, or thought-provoking?	Success!	Getting there!	Getting started!
	Next Steps:		
Were your ideas expressed...			
...using a respectful, academic writer's tone?	Success!	Getting there!	Getting started!
	Next Steps:		
...with correct spelling and other writing mechanics?	Success!	Getting there!	Getting started!
	Next Steps:		

Other Next Steps:

a Reasoning activity. While QFATs, verbal responses like partner sharing or class discussion, and written or electronic responses can all engage students with the questions listed here, certain assessment methods are better at revealing depth of thought than others.

Reasoning and creative Products are the two types of learning that are typically included the least in ensemble curricula. As a result, summative assessment should be undertaken judiciously, and only after students have had sufficient opportunity for practice and formative assessment. The learning and growth resulting from engaging students in Reasoning—or any other worthwhile pursuit—is reason enough to undertake it, whether or not it makes it into the gradebook. Examples 5.19 and 5.20 could be used for summative assessment by including a simple overall rating at the top.

Box 5.6: PERFORMING QUESTIONS

- Why do we have concerts? How are concerts different from recordings? What does that mean for our preparation?
- If your conductor had car trouble and couldn't make it to your concert, could the concert still happen? What would you have to do? Should you do any of these things even when the conductor is present?
- Out of the whole judge sheet, which categories are the most important, and why? Do you think this answer changes depending on who is answering the question? If so, how? What does this mean for us? Should we still focus on the most important categories even if they aren't worth more points?

Box 5.7: REPERTOIRE QUESTIONS

- What is special about this piece? How does it fit with the other pieces on this concert? What does that mean for me as a performer? What does that mean for my audience?
- Is it important for everyone in an ensemble to have the same interpretation of a piece? Why or why not? What should happen if there are disagreements?
- Why do composers write music? How do you suppose they react when they hear their music played? If the composer came to choir tomorrow, what might she be hoping to hear? What might she say about our performance of her piece?

Box 5.8: FUNDAMENTALS QUESTIONS

- Why is it important to have good fundamentals, intonation, or even correct notes? What would happen if we didn't work on those things? Is correctness enough for a good performance? If not, what else is required?
- The famous jazz trumpeter Miles Davis once said, "Do not fear mistakes. There are none." What do you think he meant by that?
- Do you think everyone or nearly everyone has the same idea of what "good tone" and "bad tone" are? If not, what might the differences be? Do you think there are any aspects of "good tone" or "bad tone" upon which nearly everyone would agree?

Box 5.9: MUSIC QUESTIONS

- Did you know that there is a robot that can play the trumpet? Do you think people or robots would be better at playing music? Why? What does mean for us as performers?
- If you were in charge of this choir program for a day, what would you do? Why? What if you were in charge for a year?
- French composer Claude Debussy famously stated that "music is the space between the notes." What do you think this means? How does it apply to our performance of ____?

PRODUCT ASSESSMENT

Box 5.10: PRODUCT VERBS

- Design
- Develop
- Create
- Compose
- Improvise
- Innovate

Products are students' original creations: compositions, improvisations, program notes, blog posts, and the like. Products are often touted as authentic assessment, but the evaluation criteria must be authentic to the product itself, not enabling skills. For example, a rhythm composition project in which the primary purpose is to evaluate whether students understand time signatures is a Knowledge assessment. An album review blog post is a Product if it is evaluated according to criteria for a successful album review and blog post, but it is a Knowledge target if the evaluation is focused on appropriate use of terminology.

Many musical Products involve personal motivations, tastes, and creativity. These subjectivities make Product assessment a different undertaking than assessment of Knowledge, Reasoning, and Skills. If a student has deliberately created a piece of art, who are we to judge its success? Sounds that seem "wrong" may actually be just what the composer intended.[3] However, it is possible to establish baseline criteria for an artistic creation or opinion piece. Creativity educator Maud Hickey suggests that criteria for compositions may include "logical, interesting, and feelingful,"[4] or "aesthetic appeal, creativity, and craftsmanship."[5] Other such criteria might include organization, flow, or coherence; originality; and appropriateness for the audience or venue. However, open-ended evaluation and emergent criteria (see Chapter 3) are certainly appropriate for creative Products.

Technical and stylistic conventions certainly play a role in an artifact's effectiveness at communication or representation of the creator's point of view. Music educators may feel free to establish these enabling skills as gateway criteria (see Chapter 8), allowing the summative evaluation to focus on the musicality of students' creations. Still, students who use nonstandard ideas, techniques, or formats may not be "wrong" at all but rather innovative or true to their wishes for their work. Delightful dialogue—and learning—can result from respectful inquiry into students' artistic decisions. Requiring students to submit an explanatory narrative (possibly written as program notes) along with their compositions helps the assessor to understand and evaluate them.

While they are not Products in the literal sense of being original creations, teachers may wish to include student-directed community performances as Product assessments. Students have much to gain from the process of securing a venue, recruiting peers, selecting a program, handling the logistics, and executing their own performance. One possibility for Products relevant to ensemble music is a Make Someone's Day project

Example 5.21: Composition rubric

Was the music...	YES!	Getting there!	Not yet!	Next Steps
Logical?	The organization or form was logical, intentional, or understandable.	The organization was mostly logical, intentional, and understandable.	The organization was difficult to follow, or was a hindrance to the performance.	
Interesting?	The musical ideas were fresh and interesting throughout. Any pre-existing musical material is incorporated in a fresh or interesting way.	The musical ideas were fresh and interesting most of the time.	The music does not consistently capture audience interest.	
Feelingful?	The music was feelingful, moving and artistic throughout.	The music was mostly feelingful, moving, or artistic.	The music may have been somewhat feelingful, moving, or artistic, but may not elicit a feeling reaction from most audiences.	
Well executed?	Genre, format, and presentation were all well suited for the artistic intent.	Genre, format, and presentation were well suited for the artistic intent, with some small details being seemingly out of place.	At least one of genre, format, or presentation did not appear to be well suited to the artistic intent, or may have detracted from it.	
Ms. Mueller's comments:				

(Example 5.22), in which students are assigned the authentic task of brightening someone's day with their music once per quarter. Students who complete such a project have certainly synthesized many musical abilities in an authentic performance task.

Example 5.22: Product assessment

Make Someone's Day with Music

Planning

Whose day did you choose to brighten? _____

What do you know about the person's musical preferences or traditions that could help you plan your performance? _____

_____

Explain what you plan for your musical engagement: _____

_____

_____

Reflection

Describe your musical engagement. What happened? _____

_____

_____

The next time you do this, what will you make sure to do again? _____

_____

_____

The next time you do this, what would help things go better? _____

_____

_____

DISPOSITION ASSESSMENT

Box 5.11: DISPOSITION VERBS

- Value
- Appreciate
- Feel
- Embrace
- Be
- Exemplify
- Experience

Students' values and actions are rooted in their experiences with peers, teachers, families, and society. Beliefs and feelings resulting from these experiences do not vanish when students enter the music room, and teachers are wise to acknowledge them and coach students in how to approach them. Navigating students' self-talk, beliefs about success, and emotional reactions is a key but underutilized strategy for instruction, performance, and retention in music programs. Chapter 1 mentions several assessable Dispositions, such as:

- Feelings about a particular task, piece, or event
- Performance anxiety or confidence
- Self-efficacy
- Group efficacy
- Mindset
- Attribution
- Persistence
- Motivation
- Enjoyment
- Sense of belonging

Assessment of Dispositions is fundamentally different from other types of learning targets. Disposition assessment frequently relies on honest student self-reports rather than evaluation by the teacher. There is a persistent risk of students providing answers that they think the teacher wants, or teachers misjudging students' perceived "effort" or "motivation." As Dispositions are personal and situationally specific, the goal is often not "success" but rather increased personal understanding and all of its associated benefits. Accordingly, Disposition assessment is usually best left ungraded. As outlined in Chapter 4, data-informed instruction attempts to use information about students to facilitate instruction and instructional decisions. Teachers can make their classrooms more human and more effective when they know which students don't feel accepted by peers, have performance anxiety, or don't feel challenged. Traditionally, teachers have used their intuition more than formal assessment for Dispositions. Formal assessment is not a substitute for observation and personal communication, but rather another tool in the toolbox.

Example 5.23 is a flexible format that could be used to address many Dispositions. Student names enable individualized follow-up, but these assessments can also provide honest information about the group's attitudes when done anonymously, as in Example 5.24.

Example 5.23: Disposition self assessment

How you feel is important in orchestra!	Disagree				Agree	
I feel accepted by my peers.	0	1	2	3	4	5
I feel like orchestra has a family atmosphere.	0	1	2	3	4	5
People in orchestra know my name.	0	1	2	3	4	5
People in orchestra think I am good at music.	0	1	2	3	4	5
I think I am good at playing my instrument.	0	1	2	3	4	5
I think that if I practice my instrument, I can get better.	0	1	2	3	4	5
Some people have more musical talent than others.	0	1	2	3	4	5
I try to keep my classmates from hearing me play.	0	1	2	3	4	5
I feel like I could make All-District with enough work.	0	1	2	3	4	5
I don't look forward to playing alone.	0	1	2	3	4	5
I feel like I often have bad luck on playing tests.	0	1	2	3	4	5
I like being in orchestra.	0	1	2	3	4	5
I feel happy with how our orchestra performs at concerts.	0	1	2	3	4	5
When I practice my instrument, I know how to get better.	0	1	2	3	4	5
I feel like I work harder in class than my classmates do.	0	1	2	3	4	5
I would recommend being in orchestra to my friends.	0	1	2	3	4	5
I feel like I practice more than my classmates do.	0	1	2	3	4	5
I enjoy it when we play concerts in the auditorium.	0	1	2	3	4	5
I enjoy it when we play concerts at the state festival.	0	1	2	3	4	5

Is there anything else you would like me to know about you?

Example 5.24: Choir membership disposition assessment

	Learning about music & singing	Performing at concerts & festivals	Relationships with friends in choir
How important is this to your wanting to be in choir?	0 1 2 3 4 5	0 1 2 3 4 5	0 1 2 3 4 5
Why do you say so? Please give any details you think would be helpful.			
How much do you personally want to improve on this in the coming semester?	0 1 2 3 4 5	0 1 2 3 4 5	0 1 2 3 4 5
How much do you think that I should talk about this when we visit the 5th graders?	0 1 2 3 4 5	0 1 2 3 4 5	0 1 2 3 4 5

Disposition self assessment can reveal and clarify the sources of students' emotions and anxieties, as in Example 5.25. To facilitate student engagement, teachers may also wish to have information about what kinds of music students value and what their "hidden talents" might be (Example 5.26).

Example 5.25: Performance anxiety reflection

	Singing by myself in class (not for a grade)	Singing by myself for singing tests	Singing with the choir in class	Singing with the choir in concerts
How nervous or anxious do you usually feel?	0 1 2 3 4 5	0 1 2 3 4 5	0 1 2 3 4 5	0 1 2 3 4 5
What does your brain say to you, before or while you sing?				
Is there anything you say to yourself when you sing? How does it work?				
Are you afraid anything will happen if people hear you sing? If so, what?				
How nervous are you about classmates hearing you?	0 1 2 3 4 5	0 1 2 3 4 5	0 1 2 3 4 5	0 1 2 3 4 5
How nervous are you about teachers hearing you?	0 1 2 3 4 5	0 1 2 3 4 5	0 1 2 3 4 5	0 1 2 3 4 5
How nervous are you about other audience members hearing you?	0 1 2 3 4 5	0 1 2 3 4 5	0 1 2 3 4 5	0 1 2 3 4 5
Would you like me to meet with you privately during resource time to talk about this?				

Example 5.26: Musical assets

What instruments can you play well?	
What instruments can you play a little?	
Do you play instruments outside of school? If so, tell me about it!	
Do you sing outside of school? If so, tell me about it!	
Do you write music? If so, tell me about it!	
What languages besides English can you read or speak? How fluent are you?	
What kinds of music were around your house when you were young? Tell me about genres, artists, songs, anything! Did your family make music together?	
What kinds of music do you currently listen to when you're not in class? Tell me about genres, artists, songs, anything!	

SUMMARY

Assessment and instruction in a classroom setting differ from the "rehearsal" framework traditionally employed by ensemble music teachers. Off-the-podium assessment can be the best way for teachers to gain an understanding of their students' knowledge, fundamental skills, and ability to perform repertoire. The design of an effective assessment yields the desired information about individual students, rather than generalizations about groups. Music educators can keep assessment fresh and fun for students by employing technology, creativity, and innovation to turn their existing skills at "rehearsing" into individualized assessments to promote learning.

TERMS

- On the podium
- Off the podium
- Transfer
- Graphic organizer

ACTIVITIES

5.1. Choose two contrasting musical understanding learning targets, per-haps from those you identified in Chapter 2. For both, write how you would assess student progress on that target through each lens of KRSPD. Which tasks and methods seem like the best fit?

5.2. Observe a rehearsal, or watch a video of one. Which rehearsal topics might have been facilitated by an off-the-podium strategy? How might you approach these topics?

5.3. From your experience, make a list of which musical understandings identified in this chapter are more and less commonly taught and assessed in music classes. Are there any others that are important to you?

CHAPTER 6
Fundamental Skills

You want to avoid a situation where the musicians are docile, uninvolved, and sit back and wait for your instructions and answers. This is a very difficult thing because we've got only so much time. We want to keep things moving, and we want the players to get it as fast as possible. But if they understand the concepts, they can transfer them to other situations and you won't have to reteach the same thing in a different guise; they can understand how a lot of what you do in X piece can work in Y piece.

Larry Rachleff[1]

Box 6.1: CHAPTER 6 ESSENTIAL QUESTIONS

1. How can assessment help students learn the fundamental skills of music making?
2. In what particular ways can Skill assessments be used in choir, orchestra, and band classrooms?

Skills are often at the heart of music teachers' curricular goals. While Chapter 7 is dedicated to assessment in performance preparation, the focus of this chapter is fundamentals. Music teachers often emphasize fundamentals, and with good reason. Better fundamentals mean better performers, and better performers make better ensembles.

Box 6.2: SKILL VERBS

- Play or sing
- Buzz or bow
- Demonstrate
- Clap and count
- Sight-read
- Perform
- Transcribe

Targeted assessment

As outlined in Chapter 1, musical elements are interdependent and con-text-specific. For example, intonation is affected by tessitura, location on the fingerboard, vowels, dynamics, and more. Still, in off-the-podium teaching, isolating discrete Skills enables targeted formative assessment and focused instruction. Both students and teachers can be distracted by confounders. When evaluating whether students can execute smooth crescendos and diminuendos, an excerpt that also involves fast fingers or Portuguese diction may not be the most illuminating. While students do eventually need to be able to change dynamics while using fast fingers, delaying added complexity until targeted assessment has confirmed that students have mastered the basic Skill is a shrewd use of scaffolding. Many classrooms would benefit from increased assessment of individual fundamentals—not instead of applying them, but before and alongside their application in repertoire.

In addition to a carefully selected task or excerpt, a targeted assessment helps the teacher focus on evaluating the exact skill at hand and helps the student receive the most salient feedback. While Example 6.1 is the type of assessment teachers use in many situations, the learning target of playing scales with correct key signatures is only 25 percent of the evaluation. Example 6.2 is a more valid assessment of a student's ability to play scales. When it is desirable to target a single ability, assessments can be constructed to reinforce that the assessment was of *this* intonation, not *all* intonation—particularly when an exercise or passage is idiosyncratic.[2] A criterion of "today's intonation" or "your intonation on this passage" sends a different message than "your intonation."

Example 6.1: Unfocused scale assessment

Scale	Notes	Rhythms	Tone quality	Articulation
G Major	1 2 3 4 5	1 2 3 4 5	1 2 3 4 5	1 2 3 4 5
D Major	1 2 3 4 5	1 2 3 4 5	1 2 3 4 5	1 2 3 4 5

Example 6.2: Focused scale assessment

Scale	Notes	Steadiness
G Major	__ All correct __ 1 missed: _____ __ 2+ missed: _____	__ Like a boss! __ Some hesitation __ Hard for you to get through it
D Major	__ All correct __ 1 missed: _____ __ 2+ missed: _____	__ Like a boss! __ Some hesitation __ Hard for you to get through it
Your Next Steps:		

Skill components

While they are often complex, Skills have discrete components that can be quickly assessed in a yes/no manner. One of the easiest ways for ensemble teachers to begin employing individual assessment in their classrooms is to employ checklist-type assessments for enabling skills, as in Examples 6.3 and 6.4. While this kind of assessment does not encompass everything in the curriculum, a short "watch list" can include most of the ways that students might struggle with hand position, tone production, and other fundamentals. Ask yourself: "How will they probably get it wrong?"

To reinforce the idea that Skills involve continuous improvement, teachers can organize their rating scales as a continuum or spiral that acknowledges progress and encourages continued refinement. In Example 6.5, the score divisors are organized progressively according to the student's grade. In sixth grade, a score of 12 (all 3s) is the benchmark, but all 4s is the expectation for an eighth grader. The form could be used

Example 6.3: Dynamics component assessment

You played:

	Noticeable difference?	Full, consistent sound?	In tune?	Suggestions for improvement
Loud (*forte*)				
Soft (*piano*)				
	Smooth dynamic change?	Full, consistent sound?	Stable pitch?	Suggestions for improvement
Soft to loud (*crescendo*)				
Loud to soft (*decrescendo*)				

recursively, reflecting the spiral curriculum, and easily stored as a part of student portfolios. The form could also be used formatively without a total.

Assessing individuals

Often our students are unaware of the sounds that they are actually making, attributing to themselves their peers' good tone or correct notes. The more often students sing or play alone and hear their own performance, the more realistic they can be about their development. In Assessment for Learning terms, solo playing and singing helps students answer the "Where am I now?" question. Students are most willing to sing or play alone in a supportive and nonjudgmental classroom environment. If students aren't used to performing solo, assessment of their Skills may be confounded by task unfamiliarity or performance anxiety. For this reason, chair challenges and other high-pressure endeavors should be separate from low-stakes assessment for learning.

Many teachers avoid individual performance assessment because of the class time it involves. However, there are ways to keep the class moving and still evaluate individuals. Teachers could:

Example 6.4: Jazz improvisation assessment
Adapted from Glenn Williams

	Yes! I can do this.	I can't yet, but feel OK about my progress.	Help!	Specifics:
Preparation				
I can play the roots of the chord changes from memory.				
I can play 1-2-3's from memory.				
I can play 1-3-5-7's from memory.				
I can play ascending and descending scales from memory.				
Improvisation Basics				
I can follow the chord changes when I play a solo.				
I can listen to (and stay with) the accompaniment.				
I can use notes *and rests* of various durations.				
I can connect measures and chords together to make music.				
I feel confident when I improvise.				
Improvisation Extensions				
I can remember what I played and give my solo a structure.				
I can connect my solo to the previous soloist in some way.				
I can include melodic or rhythmic sequences.				
I can use chromaticism like bebop or diminished scales.				
I can quote familiar tunes.				

- Walk through the ensemble during an exercise to hear how individuals play or sing, taking notes or using a one-item checkbox assessment.
- Set up a video camera (or tablet) in a practice room, closet, office, or hallway and teach students a simple procedure to start and stop recording; then, students get up one at a time to record while class is still meeting.
- Have students use the cameras or voice recorders on their own devices to capture their performance and send it to the teacher.
- Collect individual "selfies" to assess embouchure or vowel shapes, or take group pictures to evaluate posture or facial expression.

- Use peer assessment, possibly involving a system of mentors or other student musical leadership.
- Employ dedicated music assessment software.
- Ask their administrators if a substitute teacher or off-duty teacher's aide might be available to help.

The teacher may judiciously consider how long excerpts need to be. With a targeted task and targeted assessment tool, teachers can evaluate most Skills in just a few seconds. If a teacher only hears students singing individually once per semester, then singing tests would need to be longer,

Example 6.5: Wind tone rating scale

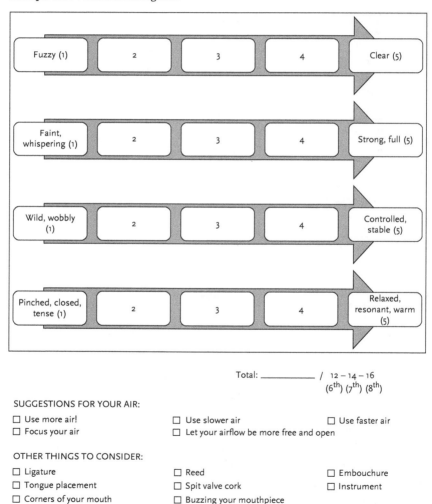

Total: _____ / 12 – 14 – 16
(6th) (7th) (8th)

SUGGESTIONS FOR YOUR AIR:

☐ Use more air!   ☐ Use slower air   ☐ Use faster air
☐ Focus your air   ☐ Let your airflow be more free and open

OTHER THINGS TO CONSIDER:

☐ Ligature   ☐ Reed   ☐ Embouchure
☐ Tongue placement   ☐ Spit valve cork   ☐ Instrument
☐ Corners of your mouth   ☐ Buzzing your mouthpiece

to incorporate a broad range of Skills. If, however, the teacher is only evaluating whether a singer can accurately sing a major and a minor triad in solfège, the assessment material can be extremely brief: "My name is Tony Wiederhold. Do, mi, sol, mi, do. La, do, mi, do, la. Thank you." Students and teachers alike will probably be more satisfied with frequent, concise, targeted assessments than lengthy comprehensive ones.

Self and peer Skill assessment

Self assessment and peer assessment can also help to keep students playing or singing as much as possible. The more support teachers provide, the more successful students' evaluations will be. Self assessment, such as Example 6.6, is straightforward and effective. The "Reasoning assessment" section in Chapter 5 introduces methods for focused listening and critique. Example 6.7 is another way for students could participate in guided peer assessment. Students typically find this process stimulating, and take it seriously when there is enough support and structure to help them do it well. Peer assessment using QFATs or simple paper or electronic written responses can also be engaging and informative. Many stable or rotating student groupings are possible, including partners, sections, chamber ensembles, and light-hearted attributes like birth month or shirt color.

If teachers want or need to assess students individually while everyone is in the same room, there are ways to make that more engaging as well. One method is to employ the "solo/soli" approach, where everyone plays or sings a passage or exercise together, then one student performs alone, then everyone performs together again, then the next student performs alone,

Example 6.6: Simple self assessment

Scale (concert pitch)	Memorized	Know it	Sort of know it	Don't know it
C				
F				
B♭				
E♭				
A♭				
D♭				

Example 6.7: Guided peer assessment

How Does My Bae Play Today?

Student #1 name: _____

Student #2 name: _____

What you are playing: _____

Student #1 plays; Student #2 listens and evaluates

Did your partner seem confident?	YES	MOSTLY	NOT REALLY	NOT SURE
Did your partner play with a full sound?	YES	MOSTLY	NOT REALLY	NOT SURE
Did your partner keep the bow straight?	YES	MOSTLY	NOT REALLY	NOT SURE
Could your partner play it without stopping?	YES	MOSTLY	NOT REALLY	NOT SURE
Did your partner play without stopping the bow?	YES	MOSTLY	NOT REALLY	NOT SURE

What's one thing your partner is doing well?

What's one thing your partner could do to improve?

Student #2 plays; Student #1 listens and evaluates

Did your partner seem confident?	YES	MOSTLY	NOT REALLY	NOT SURE
Did your partner play with a full sound?	YES	MOSTLY	NOT REALLY	NOT SURE
Did your partner keep the bow straight?	YES	MOSTLY	NOT REALLY	NOT SURE
Could your partner play it without stopping?	YES	MOSTLY	NOT REALLY	NOT SURE
Did your partner play without stopping the bow?	YES	MOSTLY	NOT REALLY	NOT SURE

What's one thing your partner is doing well?

What's one thing your partner could do to improve?

---

and so on. One student could perform while others pizzicato, finger, conduct, or hand-sign along. One student could perform while others serve as the metronome by counting the subdivision aloud. Randomization can add student interest; a colleague of mine used to draw students' names out of the "Box of Destiny." The more engaging formative assessment is, the more willingly students will participate. The more familiar the procedures are, the more efficient the process will become.

The next several sections contain examples designed for particular teaching contexts, but readers may find the underlying thought processes to be broadly applicable. The basic building blocks of technique and musicianship are explicit goals of beginner classes, but teachers are wise not to assume that their older students already have strong technique. Assessment of fundamentals benefits students of all ages. As most of these assessments are analytic rather than holistic, they are best used formatively.

MUSIC READING

Music reading is an important Skill in many ensemble classes. Music reading instruction and assessment is nearly always best when it is separate from performance repertoire. Literature that students can learn over weeks or months is almost certainly more demanding than what they can sight-read today. Especially in instrumental ensembles, some students have parts that vary little from piece to piece. And, the nature of performance literature does not allow for easy differentiation. However, differentiation is critical. Experienced teachers know that technique and literacy develop differently, and there is usually a wide range of reading abilities in a given classroom.

As with many skills, music reading has several enablers that can be assessed separately or simultaneously. What music teachers often want students to be able to do with sight-reading centers on notes and rhythms. To be sure, reading rhythms or notes separately does not imply the ability to read them together, or apply style or expression. Still, as it is easier to determine Next Steps when skills are assessed in isolation, targeted prompting material and assessment criteria make formative feedback easier to deliver and absorb.

Teachers can develop their own sight-reading or sight-singing materials, and many are commercially available. Sorting exercises into groups or stages (or playful levels like martial arts belts) facilitates both assessment and differentiation. Table 6.1 contains a sample organizational structure

Table 6.1: SAMPLE BEGINNING BAND MUSIC LITERACY LEVELS

Level	Notes	Major key signatures	Rhythms (simple meter)	Rhythms (compound meter)
Newbie	B♭, C, D			
Apprentice	E♭, F	B♭		
Master	E♮, low A♮	F, C		
Grand Master	G, high A♭, high B♭	E♭		
Legend	D♭, high A♮, high C	A♭		

(but certainly not a definitive one) for beginning band; choral educators might choose to list solfège patterns and starting pitches instead. Students will likely be at different levels with, say, notes and compound rhythms. If a student is a "Master" with notes but an "Apprentice" with compound

Example 6.8: Generic music reading evaluation

All of the **pitches** were correct	Developing	Beginning	Comments:
All of the **rhythmic values** were correct	Developing	Beginning	Comments:
The **tempo** was consistent throughout, without stops or hesitation	Developing	Beginning	Comments:
The music was performed **confidently**	Developing	Beginning	Comments:

Example 6.9: Clap and count assessment no. 1

The rhythms you clapped...	were all correct	were mostly correct	showed that you need more practice
SPECIFICS:			
Your tempo today...	was consistent	changed noticeably	was hard to follow
SPECIFICS:			
The beat numbers...	were all correct	were mostly correct	showed that you need more practice
SPECIFICS:			
Your Next Steps are:			

Example 6.10: Clap and count assessment no. 2

The subdivision you counted...

_____ was confidently counted out loud   _____ could be louder or more confident

_____ had a rock-solid tempo   _____ could be more consistent

_____ used the appropriate syllables   _____ was hampered by syllables

The rhythms you clapped...

_____ were all correct   _____ were mostly correct

_____ showed that you need more practice   _____ were hard to hear

_____ lined up with your subdivision   _____ need to line up with the subdivision

Your Next Steps are:

Example 6.11: Pitch-matching assessment

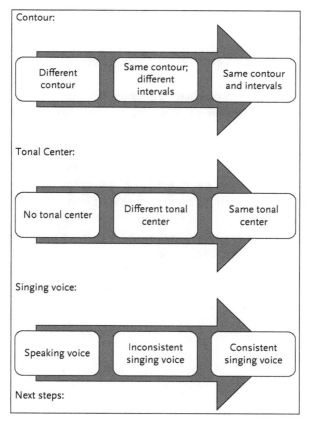

FUNDAMENTAL SKILLS [123]

Example 6.12: Sight-singing assessment

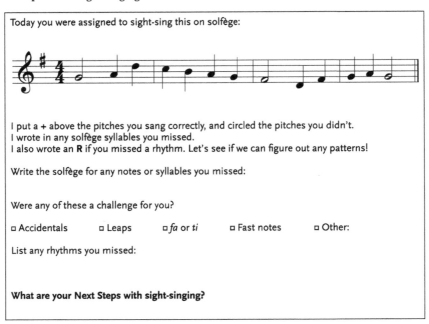

Today you were assigned to sight-sing this on solfège:

I put a + above the pitches you sang correctly, and circled the pitches you didn't.
I wrote in any solfège syllables you missed.
I also wrote an **R** if you missed a rhythm. Let's see if we can figure out any patterns!

Write the solfège for any notes or syllables you missed:

Were any of these a challenge for you?

□ Accidentals   □ Leaps   □ *fa* or *ti*   □ Fast notes   □ Other:

List any rhythms you missed:

What are your Next Steps with sight-singing?

rhythms, the Next Steps are evident. Class trends can also facilitate data-informed instruction.

Teachers accomplish individual sight-reading assessment in many ways. A level system allows differentiation—the teacher could pull exercises out of one of several literal or proverbial hats depending on the student's needs. Students might "level up" with three consecutive successful evaluations done with a tool similar to Example 6.8. The subsequent examples represent additional possibilities for assessment of music reading skills. Teachers might use Examples 6.9 or 6.10 depending on whether they have students say rhythm syllables or beat numbers when they have students clap rhythms. Example 6.11 is for pitch matching in a beginning or children's choir setting, and Example 6.12 is a more advanced sight-singing assessment with a student reflection component. All music literacy skills require enabling factual, conceptual, and procedural Knowledge, as introduced in Chapter 5. "Leveling up" could require Knowledge as well as Skills. Many sensible systems are possible.

STRING EXAMPLES

As string educators know, string playing's enabling skills are numerous and exacting. Fortunately, orchestra classrooms have the advantages of all technique being visible and commonalities in technique across the instruments. The nature of string technique lends itself well to checklist-type assessment; there are just a lot of items to check. The examples in this section are not intended to be comprehensive or aligned with any particular approach or sequence. Teachers who adapt them using their everyday instructional language will give feedback that is more comprehensible to students. Example 6.18 could be extended to other strings and positions. Example 6.19 could be modified by changing the focus to bow weight or placement. Repeating the exercise with contrasting musical material can support students' understanding of how technique facilitates musicianship.

Example 6.13: String posture and position assessment

	Looking good!	Let's work on this!	Your Next Steps:
Foot position (standing)			
Body position			
Instrument position			
Bow arm			
Bow hold			
Bow placement			
Left hand			

Example 6.14: Bowing assessment

	Proficient	Developing	Beginning	Your Next Steps:
Placement				
Bow angle				
Weight				
Elbow angle				
Speed				
Direction				

Example 6.15: Violin bow hold assessment

	You do it without reminders	You can do it with a reminder	You aren't there yet	Your Next Steps:
Index finger on ferrule				
Bent thumb on frog's nose				
Middle fingers draped				
Pinky on top and curved				
Hand pronated				
Wrist & fingers relaxed				

Example 6.16: Performance injury screener

How often do you feel pain, tingles, or numbness when you play?			
	Never ☺	Sometimes 😐	Often ☹
My neck			
My back			
My jaw			
My right shoulder			
My right elbow			
My right wrist			
My right fingers			
My left shoulder			
My left elbow			
My left wrist			
My left fingers			
My left sixth toe (...*just in case*)			

Example 6.17: String technique assessment

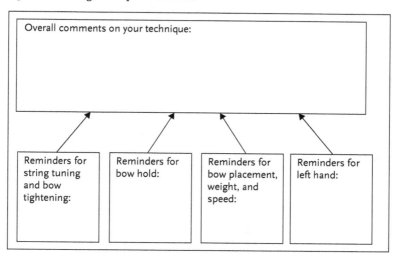

Example 6.18: Second finger assessment

Example 6.19: Bow distribution peer assessment

Bow Distribution Partner Activity

Step 1: Decide which person is GREEN and who is GOLD.

    Write the name of the GREEN person: _____

    Write the name of the GOLD person: _____

Step 2: Write how you think measures 1 through 4 of *Fiddler's Hoedown* should sound:

    _____

    _____

Step 3: Each person plays measures 1-4, using the <u>**lower third**</u> of the bow. GREEN person plays first.

    Write two words to describe the tone your partner made.

    _____   _____

    Did your partner's bow stay straight? *(circle one.)*   YES!   NOT TODAY

Step 4: Each person plays again, using the <u>**middle third**</u> of the bow. GOLD person plays first.

    Write two words to describe the tone your partner made.

    _____   _____

    Did your partner's bow stay straight? *(circle one.)*   YES!   NOT TODAY

Step 5: Each person plays again, using the <u>**upper third**</u> of the bow. GREEN person plays first.

    Write two words to describe the tone your partner made.

    _____   _____

    Did your partner's bow stay straight? *(circle one.)*   YES!   NOT TODAY

Step 6: Can you and your partner agree on the part of the bow that makes the best sound for the beginning of *Fiddler's Hoedown*? Write what you think it should be.

    _____

Step 7: Nicely tell your partner about any parts of the bow that could have been straighter today. ☺ Ask your partner to play them again and see if it gets better.

CHOIR EXAMPLES

It comes as no surprise that assessing or even describing voices is a complex endeavor. Voices are less straightforwardly "correct" or "incorrect" than instruments, and are unique and personal to the singer. Rather than being focused on "fixing problems," assessment can help students understand and control their voices and know which ways of singing are most germane in which situations. Examples 6.20 and 6.21 are graphic organizers for vocal classification. The teacher could classify students' most comfortable or "natural" voices (if there is such a thing) to establish a baseline. Singers could then use different symbols to mark "where they are going" with vocal tone for each piece. There are also elements of vocal technique that benefit many students. Assessment, such as Examples 6.22 through 6.26, can highlight these elements and prompt differentiated voice instruction. Prompting ranges should be comfortable for each singer, varying according to age and voice part.

Example 6.20: Vocal tone classification.
Adapted from, Henry H. Leck, and Steven Rickards. *Vocal Techniques for the Young Singer*. Indianapolis, IN: Colla Voce, 2000.

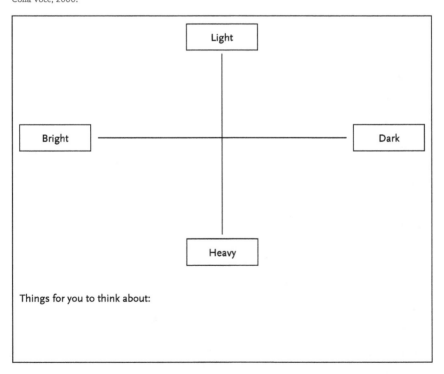

Light

Bright — Dark

Heavy

Things for you to think about:

Example 6.21: Singing voice assessment
Adapted from Scott McCoy, *Your Voice: The Basics* (Gahanna, OH: Inside View, 2016)

> Everyone's voice is unique. Voices can be described in many ways. Every voice is wonderful. Your voice is wonderful. <u>Your voice is you!!</u>
>
> This form is designed to give you a "picture" of your voice. There are no rights or wrongs on this page. We sometimes adjust our voices depending on the piece. If your voice is naturally bright, then if we want a darker sound on a particular piece, we will work on how to do that.
>
> | Bright | ←————————————→ | Dark |
> | Forward | ←————————————→ | Back |
> | Clear | ←————————————→ | Breathy |
> | Clean | ←————————————→ | Raspy |
> | Nasal | ←————————————→ | Non-nasal |
> | Vibrating | ←————————————→ | Straight tone |
> | Healthy | ←————————————→ | Health concern |
>
> Comments:

Example 6.22: Vocal technique assessment
Note: Experts in voice pedagogy differ in how they label registers. I have used the familiar "head voice" and "chest voice" here, but teachers are encouraged to use the labels of their choice.

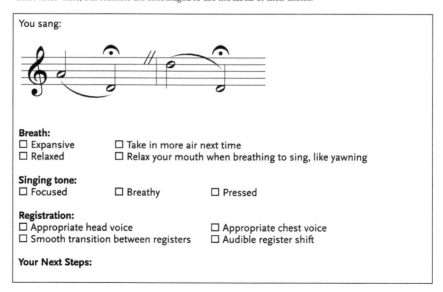

You sang:

Breath:
☐ Expansive   ☐ Take in more air next time
☐ Relaxed   ☐ Relax your mouth when breathing to sing, like yawning

Singing tone:
☐ Focused   ☐ Breathy   ☐ Pressed

Registration:
☐ Appropriate head voice   ☐ Appropriate chest voice
☐ Smooth transition between registers   ☐ Audible register shift

Your Next Steps:

Example 6.23: Singing posture assessment

	You do it without reminders	You can do it with a reminder	You aren't there yet	Your Next Steps:
Feet shoulder-width apart				
Knees loose				
Spine elongated				
Shoulders relaxed				
Chin level				
Hands relaxed at sides				

Example 6.24: Vowels assessment

Adapted from Weston Noble. *Creating the Special World: A Collection of Lectures by Weston H. Noble.* Edited by Steven M Demorest. Chicago: GIA, 2005.

Bright vowels	Dark vowels	That's how we do it!	Not today!	Your Next Steps:
[a] "ah" (bother)				
[æ] "a" (back)				
	[ʊ] "aw" (bawl)			
[ɛ] "eh" (bed)				
	[ʌ] "u" (but)			
[e] "ei" (bay)				
	[ō] "o" (boat)			
[I] "ih" (bit)				
	[ʊ] "oo" (book)			
[ē] "ee" (beet)				
	[oo] "ooh" (boot)			

Open ↓ Closed

Example 6.25: Vocal technique assessment

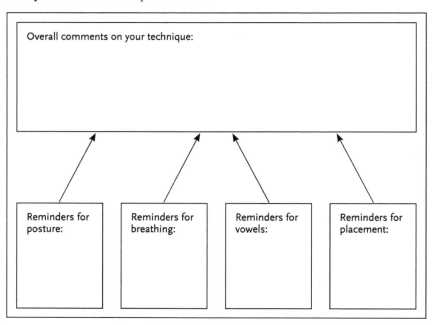

Example 6.26: Vocal health screener

	Good for you!	Some concern	Serious concern
How much sleep do you get in a typical night?	8+ hours	6–7 hours	Under 6 hours
How many non-caffeinated drinks do you have per day?	5 or more	3–4	2 or fewer
How many caffeinated drinks do you have per day?	2 or fewer	3–4	5 or more
How many times per week do you feel hoarse, or like your voice is tired?	0	1–2	3 or more
List any activities (besides this class) that require extensive use of your voice:			

Example 6.27: Part security assessment

You sang your part correctly throughout.	Your got pulled off of your part at times.	Today you had a hard time holding your part.
Details:		
Next Steps:		

Example 6.28: Performance presentation assessment.

Adapted from Cynthia Bayt Bradford, "Sound Assessment Practices in the Standards-Based Choral Curriculum," *Choral Journal* 43, no. 9 (2003): 21–27. Copyright American Choral Directors Association. Used with Permission.

	Artist	Performer	Beginner
Eyes	Communicating with director and audience	Focused on director	Wandering or looking down
Face	Confidently and appropriately engaged with music	Pleasant or relaxed	Deadpan or uninvolved
Posture and body	Singing posture; body appropriately engaged with music	Balanced and relaxed posture helpful for singing	Slouched, slumped, or unbalanced
Hands and arms	Appropriately engaged with music	Relaxed at sides	Fidgeting or crossed
Comments and Next Steps:			

For part-singing assessment, independence is a fundamental consideration. While it would be ideal for all singers to be able to sing their parts in isolation, valid assessment will mirror rehearsal conditions. In class, some teachers have students sing in quartets or other small groups. Part-singing assessment is still possible outside of class, however. Students can record themselves at home, using a prompting recording of the accompaniment or even their part from a practice track. Students can also be assigned to do at-home recording with a partner or friend. In class, teachers could assess students' ability to hold a part securely as its own skill. Students could learn a partner song or canon and sing it as a duet; teachers might use an evaluation similar to Example 6.27 that is quick to complete.

BAND EXAMPLES

Band classrooms have the largest number of different instruments, each with its own technique. Band is the teaching situation in which the teacher is most likely to face instruments that are somewhat unfamiliar. Well-conceived assessment can provide a template for evaluation and feed-back on each instrument's peculiarities. Teachers can consult colleagues, method books, private teachers, and other resources to determine criteria and how success is defined. Checkbox Next Steps can provide students with the exact language of a master pedagogue on that instrument, without the risk of the teacher forgetting what to say.

Teachers can use many formats for assessment of fundamentals in band. Sometimes, the same form can be used for many instruments, such as Example 6.29. To account for differences, teachers can also generate similarly formatted assessments with specific content. Example 6.30 has two sections that can stay the same for all wind instruments; each instrument can have its own characteristics under the "embouchure" heading. Many teachers have a preferred way of teaching techniques for each instrument. The precise wording is not the focus in these examples. Assessment should use the language with which students in each classroom are most familiar.

Example 6.29: Wind tone assessment

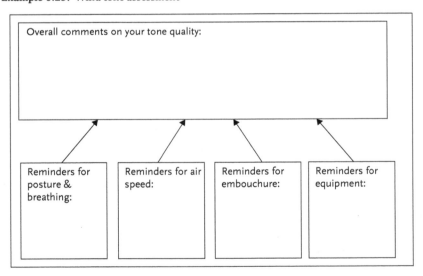

Example 6.30: Siren buzzing assessment

	Yes!	Let's work on this!	Your Next Steps:
Your posture helps you play your best			
You held and placed the mouthpiece properly			
You took a full breath			
The sound was full going up and down			
The pitch changed smoothly			
You can buzz a wide range of notes			

Example 6.31: Bassoon assessment

Bassoon Playing Assessment

Equipment (not graded)	Yes!	Not today	
You have a quality instrument	_____	_____	
All of the keys close; all pads seal	_____	_____	
You are playing on a good reed	_____	_____	
You can assemble the bassoon on your own	_____	_____	
You know at least one good bassoon joke	_____	_____	

Posture & Breathing	Yes!	Almost	Not today
You sit tall	_____	_____	_____
You keep your feet flat on the floor	_____	_____	_____
You position your instrument correctly	_____	_____	_____
You have correct and relaxed fingers and hands	_____	_____	_____
You take a big, relaxed breath	_____	_____	_____
You are blowing air at the correct speed	_____	_____	_____

Embouchure	Yes!	Almost	Not today
Your lips are rolled slightly over your teeth	_____	_____	_____
Your jaw makes a slight overbite	_____	_____	_____
Your lips make a tight "drawstring" seal	_____	_____	_____
½ to ☐ of the reed is in your mouth	_____	_____	_____

Things to remember:

Example 6.32: Brass embouchure assessment

	Success!	Not yet	Your Next Steps:
Puckered smile			
Firm corners			
Teeth apart			
Mouthpiece centered			
Full buzzzzzzz!			

Example 6.33: Clarinet embouchure assessment

	That's it!	Not quite	Your Next Steps:
Your bottom lip is rolled and stretched over your teeth			
Your chin is pointed and flat			
Your top teeth touch the mouthpiece			
The corners of your mouth are forward, like you are saying "ooh"			
Your lips make a tight, even seal around the mouthpiece			
Your tongue is arched or high, like you are saying "eee"			
Your right thumb exerts gentle upward pressure against the thumb rest			

Example 6.34: Snare drum assessment

	You do it without reminders	You can do it with a reminder	You aren't there yet	Your Next Steps:
You stand tall with your feet shoulder-width apart				
The drum head is parallel with the ground				
The stand is positioned so that the drum head is near your waist				
Your elbows are even with or slightly ahead of your body				
You hold the stick about ¼ of the way up				
Your thumbs are parallel with the stick				
Your thumbs and index fingers are gripping the stick				
Your index finger thumbnails point at the floor, and your thumbnails face each other				
Your sticks form about a right angle				

Example 6.35: Note learning assessment

Note	You can show the fingering		You can play it		You can control it		YOU KNOW THIS NOTE!
B♭	——	+	——	+	——	=	——
C	——	+	——	+	——	=	——
D	——	+	——	+	——	=	——
E♭	——	+	——	+	——	=	——
F	——	+	——	+	——	=	——
E♮	——	+	——	+	——	=	——
Low A♭	——	+	——	+	——	=	——
G	——	+	——	+	——	=	——
High A♭	——	+	——	+	——	=	——
High A♮	——	+	——	+	——	=	——
High B♭	——	+	——	+	——	=	——

Example 6.36: Band posture assessment

	You do it without reminders	You can do it with a reminder	You aren't there yet	Your Next Steps:
Heels on the floor				
Using the front of the chair				
Sitting tall				
Neck straight				
Comfortable instrument position				
Fingers slightly curved				

Example 6.37: Style assessment

Staccato Style		Legato Style
	Does it mean separated or connected?	
	Wind players: do your lungs stop & start, or blow air continuously?	
	Wind players: which syllable do you use when tonguing?	
	What are some more adjectives that we can use to describe this style?	
	What are some problems we commonly encounter when playing in this style?	
	Which piece(s) that we are currently playing use this style?	

SUMMARY

Assessment of fundamentals is facilitated by targeting a particular Skill and evaluating students individually. These exercises are only a fraction of the possible assessments in these teaching contexts. Designing any Skill assessment involves considering steps, enablers, and common stumbles, and choosing an appropriate format. Teachers can consult any available resource to identify possible elements for assessment. In the next chapter, the focus will turn to what most music teachers already do every day: assessment during the course of performance preparation. Incorporating assessment principles can lead to ensemble rehearsals that are efficient, effective, educative, and satisfying.

ACTIVITIES

6.1. Make a list of common enabling skills that have arisen in your teaching. How might you assess students' mastery of these skills?

6.2. Choose any performance skill and develop an analytic rubric for it. Think through common feedback items and include them as checkboxes. Finally, creative a holistic summative assessment involving your skill.

6.3. Choose an example assessment from this chapter. Revise or adapt it to your teaching situation.

CHAPTER 7

Concert Preparation

One can educate orchestras and one can educate choruses, but ultimately, one should not [merely] conduct them. . . . Ultimately you educate them to do the performance within themselves.

Robert Shaw

Box 7.1: CHAPTER 7 ESSENTIAL QUESTIONS

1. How can rehearsals and concerts be viewed through an assessment lens?
2. How can music teachers use assessment strategies when rehearsing concert repertoire on the podium?
3. How can music teachers use assessment strategies when assessing concert repertoire off the podium?

ARE CONCERTS ASSESSMENTS?

Performing is an integral part of ensemble music. Concerts are exciting; they are sharing opportunities; they are motivators; they are sources of pride for students, families, school, and community; they are important musical experiences. However, the primary purpose of a performance is to display, not evaluate, what individual students have learned. Of course, important information results from performances. Teachers can use recordings and judge sheets to identify Next Steps for their ensembles and for their own instruction. In that sense, concerts are assessment. This raises an important question: assessment of *what*?

Concerts are group, not individual, activities. In most cases, it's difficult to say which children made which sounds. No matter how much we would like them to be, ensemble performances are not assessment of individual students. This means that they are not a defensible basis for grades (see Chapter 8). Concerts, festivals, and competitions can be seen as summative assessment of certain attributes of a music *program*, but they cannot evaluate how much students have grown, musical understandings and abilities beyond the narrow range involved, or disparities between schools. While most teachers and students do their best to prepare for performances, music programs operate within the bounds of school size, resources, instructional time, and other factors outside of their control. Consequently, ratings from competitions and festivals are also dubious data for teacher evaluation.[1]

Even though concerts have limited value as student assessment, they are still cornerstones of ensemble music. Therefore, **performance preparation assessment** (PPA) is a type of assessment that has universal applicability. This chapter will focus on strategies that can transform this core function of ensemble music education.

WHAT *IS* A REHEARSAL?

When music teachers talk about **rehearsal**, they typically mean a setting in which a full ensemble works on repertoire for an upcoming performance. A school rehearsal frequently mirrors a rehearsal in a collegiate or professional ensemble. The Maestro teacher says, "Home is where you learn your part—rehearsal is where you come to learn everyone else's part." The Maestro says, "Violins, you need to practice the end." The assumption is that the performers possess enough skills and understandings to "come to rehearsal with your parts prepared" and that any misunderstanding or inability results from a lack of commitment or work ethic. These are reasonable expectations for professional musicians. But what if our assumptions about students' ability to work independently are faulty? How would we know? Teachers usually have an extensive repertory of rehearsal strategies for helping students master various difficulties. How does the teacher know which students need help with which musical elements in which sections of which pieces?

The answers to these questions lie in assessment. Teachers may address sections or the full ensemble or provide vague instructions such as "You need to work on this," because their assessment practices haven't provided them with specific information about individuals' Skills with the performance repertoire and underlying Knowledge, Reasoning, fundamental Skills, or Dispositions that are the hidden causes of the symptoms the teacher sees. Even while standing on a podium and working toward a performance, thinking like an off-the-podium teacher and assessor can result in a great performance this time *and* better musicians for next time.

Some ensemble music educators resist thinking more like a teacher on a podium and less like a Maestro. Ramona Wis writes, "As conductors we often experience an internal conflict when it comes to thinking of ourselves as teachers. . . . Instead of thinking of ourselves as teachers we prefer to be thought of as *artists*: creative, talented, and unique professionals."[2] Still, whether or not we see ourselves primarily as teachers, students who do not know how to accomplish our goals will be challenged to accomplish them. Applying "teacher" thinking rather than Maestro thinking to rehearsal situations is a student-oriented pathway to fine performances. There is a balance to be found between teaching off the podium and teaching from the podium, influenced by student experience level, amount of time before the performance, and countless other considerations. The question is not which instructional modes or methods to employ, but when to use them. This chapter is not a collection of rehearsal strategies per se; many excellent rehearsal resources are already available. Rather, these are ideas to help music educators use the teaching and assessment strategies from previous chapters to augment what they already do on the podium.

INFORMAL ASSESSMENT ON THE PODIUM

Elements from each of the preceding chapters translate directly to teaching from the podium. Many music teachers feel comfortable using learning targets and assessment for fundamentals, but less so when it comes to PPA. Students benefit when teachers approach concert preparation like any other learning goal: a cumulative series of understandings and abilities that gradually come together in the form of the performance on the stage. Of course, a musically satisfying performance is more than an additive function of measure 1 plus measure 2 through the end. Nonetheless, school ensemble concert preparation inherently involves teaching students to understand and perform together, balancing granular concerns with the big picture and feeling efficacious during the inevitable stumbles along the way. As such, "assessment thinking" is a good frame of mind both off and on the podium. If teaching without assessment is "teaching blind," what does that mean for rehearsing without adequate information about where students are with the repertoire?

Chapter 1 referenced the "whole versus parts" dilemma in music. The same issue arises with individual musicians' contributions to a performance; the performances of this flutist and that flutist are separate but obviously related. Still, the ensemble performance is entirely dependent on its individual members. Much is lost when we think about what "the basses" are doing rather than what Meredith, Patrick, Anna, and George are doing. In addition, there are no "group" Dispositions. Each student has her own preference, nervousness, motivation, and self-efficacy for each piece. Thus, in PPA, a focus on individuals is warranted.

PPA and Assessment for Learning

The Assessment for Learning questions from Chapter 3 are relevant to performance preparation. Ensemble feedback tends to focus on where students are and sometimes where they are going, but less often how to get there. "How to get there" is frequently a question of some enabling skill or understanding and is the most important of the three AfL questions. "Where students are" is often the least important piece of information, often feels like criticism, and can often be left unsaid. What's wrong doesn't matter as much as what to do about it. Consider the examples of rehearsal feedback in Box 7.2.

Box 7.2: REHEARSAL FEEDBACK AND ASSESSMENT FOR LEARNING

"You're rushing! Don't rush!" (*Sort of answers "Where am I now?"*)

"In this passage, when you have two eighth notes together, you are rushing through them." (*"Where am I now?"*)

"In this passage, when you have two eighth notes together, you are rushing through them. Let's make sure the tempo stays the same throughout." (*"Where am I now?"* + *"Where am I going?"*)

"In this passage, when you have two eighth notes together, you are rushing through them. Let's make sure the tempo stays the same throughout. Everyone, let's count the beat division out loud and clap the rhythm . . . Now, let's perform it and *think* the beat division." (*"Where am I now?"* + *"Where am I going?"* + *"How do I get there?"*)

"Let's make sure the tempo stays the same throughout. Everyone, let's count the beat division out loud and clap the rhythm, paying careful attention to groups of two paired eighth notes . . . Now, let's perform it and *think* the beat division, especially with those eighth notes!" (*"Where am I going?"* + *"How do I get there?"*)

Teachers are wise to employ diagnostic and formative assessment of both the performance product and enabling knowledge and skills throughout the rehearsal process. Rehearsal instructions can then become descriptive "feedforward" to the ensemble, including Next Steps specifying not just what to improve but how to improve. In fact, with attention to individual abilities, enabling skills and understandings, and descriptive feedback, rehearsals are the kind of formative assessment that should be the envy of teachers in all other subjects. As with all formative assessment, rehearsals featuring low stakes and an encouraging atmosphere facilitate learning goals (i.e., trying to grow as musicians). High stakes lead students to prioritize performance goals (i.e., trying to avoid displeasing the teacher or being embarrassed in front of peers) instead. Students only "fake it" when they have something to lose.

Rehearsing like an assessor

There is usually no shortage of information input on the podium. The issue is how to organize, process, and retain the mountain of data that rehearsals generate. It's easy to notice something in the first half of a performance of a piece, only to have forgotten it by the end. Organizing and processing information is easier when the information is collected for a specific purpose, as the next sections will describe. Teachers need a system for retention of their collected information, and it doesn't have to be fancy. Simply taking notes on a paper or electronic notepad during the course of a class, or inserting sticky notes or sticky flags into the score, will ensure that nothing is overlooked. Many teachers find it easier to assess and solve problems when they move around the room to be physically nearer whoever is singing or playing. Finally, nearly everyone is better at processing information without the added cognitive load of conducting. If students don't need the baton, put it down.

Perceptive listening and error detection are easier when the teacher has a specific musical element (note accuracy, releases, style, or anything else) in mind, especially when the relevant detail is isolated. The assessment task in rehearsals is defined by *who* is performing (which individuals or section), *what* they are performing (which measures), and *how* they are performing it (as written or using scaffolding strategies like slower tempo, text only, or clap and count). Chosen well, these considerations can reveal the support or corrections students need. An effective strategy for rehearsal choices is to consider which enabling skills may be the source of an issue the teacher is hearing. For example, why are the saxophones playing wrong notes? Just forgot? New fingering? Don't understand that accidentals last until a bar line? Diagnosing and addressing underlying causes is almost certain to achieve better results than simply (and vaguely) exhorting students to focus or "be committed" or "remember the key signature." Students may misunderstand the same concept for different reasons. Individual assessment enables teachers to work with each musician in the most helpful way possible—differentiated instruction at its finest.

An intriguing way to understand the structure of segments in a rehearsal is the **rehearsal frame**[3] pictured in figure 7.1, an application of the assessment cycle and feedback loop found in earlier chapters. A rehearsal frame begins when the teacher identifies a target and ends when she or he changes the focus. The rehearsal frame concept makes it clear how deeply assessment is embedded into ensemble music, and a series of rehearsal frames is as good a blueprint as any for an effective rehearsal. Although overly prescriptive approaches to teaching are generally unhelpful, a healthy percentage of recommendations I make to teachers stem from skipping one or more steps in this process or changing the focus before a frame is complete. In particular, assessment of the decontextualized target before moving on to the full ensemble or the next target is a critical puzzle piece for effective rehearsals. Time spent providing feedback but neglecting to assess whether students actually implemented it is often wasted.

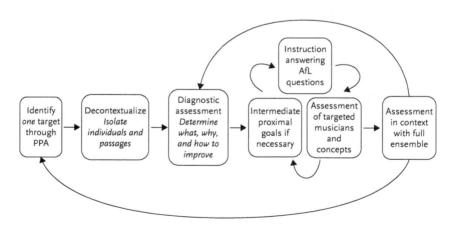

Figure 7.1: Assessment-focused rehearsal frame diagram

Adapted from Robert A. Duke, "Measures of Instructional Effectiveness in Music Research," Bulletin of the Council for Research in Music Education 143 (Winter 1999/2000): 1–48. Permission granted by the School of Music, University of Illinois.

Box 7.3: ASSESSMENT-INSPIRED PODIUM TIPS

- Regard your group as a collection of individuals. Listen to individual students as often as possible.
- Assume that students' errors are caused by a lack of enabling skills or understandings rather than lack of practice, effort, or commitment.
- Ensure feedback includes Next Steps. Always say how to do what you are asking the ensemble to do. Next Steps should be within the student's ZPD where it is, not where it "should be." Provide scaffolding, not scolding, for students who need it.
- Think of yourself as a detective or diagnostician. Look for an off-the-podium solution—likely improving students' abilities with one or more enabling skills—to any persistent problem.
- Promote self-efficacy and growth mindset by characterizing failure as a natural step in the learning process, celebrating small successes, and reinforcing that anything students can't do is something they can't do *yet*.

FORMAL ASSESSMENT OFF THE PODIUM

Full ensembles

Concert preparation does not have to be limited to the podium. Any of the methods from Chapters 3 and 4 could be employed in the service of PPA. While teachers may primarily think of Skill assessment during performance preparation, it is wise to remember that other methods may be the best way to assess underlying enablers, as in Example 7.1. Several principles from Chapters 5 and 6 are relevant to formal PPA. Frequent, targeted assessment allows the use of the results in the rehearsals that follow, and can direct students' efforts both inside and outside of class when Next Steps are provided (a productive use of data-informed instruction). Checkbox comments can be used for frequently given feedback. Assessment can also help to foster growth mindsets. Examples 7.2 and 7.3 are straightforward forms for PPA that educators can easily adapt. As they are formative and focused on Next Steps, quantitative feedback is unnecessary. Example 7.4 is a rubric that is designed for difficult technical passages, exclusively evaluating note accuracy and tempo. If students themselves decide the minimum standard for being in the performance, it is simpler to encourage them to retake the playing test until they are proficient. They almost always make the right choice.

Example 7.1: Enabling understanding assessment

Fall Concert Articulations

	Mighty Towers	Heartstrings	Into the Sunset (opening fanfare)	Into the Sunset ("Exuberantly")
In general, is the style heavy, light, or both?				
So...will we mainly use a "D" or "T" tongue?				
In general, is the style separated, connected, or both?				
So...will we mainly use an "ot" or "ah" ending?				
WHICH ARTICULATIONS WILL WE USE MOST FOR THIS PIECE?				

Example 7.2: Simple repertoire assessment no. 1

Name: _____ Piece: _____ Date: _____

Today's **completely ungraded** assessment focused on measures _____. I am giving you information about how the following musical elements affected your performance today, and what your Next Steps might be. Success doesn't come from luck or genetics; it comes from working on the right things!

Musical element	What I noticed, and where I noticed it the most	Your Next Steps for improvement

Other comments and Next Steps:

Chamber music

Chamber music is a common element in performance ensemble curricula. Teachers may intend for students to improve ensemble skills like blend, but they often spend most of their time learning parts. To focus instruction

Example 7.3: Simple repertoire assessment no. 2

Piece and passage	Where are you today?	Next Steps & practice strategies
	___ Ready for the concert ___ Almost ready for the concert, except: ___ Not yet ready for the concert, because:	

Example 7.4: PPA rubric

			You played most of the notes correctly but had several that were incorrect. **You're on the way!**	You don't yet understand enough of the notes to play it correctly. **Keep working!**
NOTES	You played all of the notes accurately. **Bravo!**	You played nearly all of the notes accurately. **Almost there!**		
TEMPO/ FLUENCY	You can play it smoothly on the first try. **Bravo!**	You can play through it but you have a few pauses and/or stumbles. **Almost there!**	You can play through it but you have several pauses and/or stumbles. **You're on the way!**	You currently struggle to get through it. **Keep working!**
Next Steps	1. Practice to cement what you have learned. 2. Be helpful and encouraging to your classmates. **3. Be a leader. Play confidently & musically!**	1. Identify areas that you need to improve. 2. Work on those small spots and then put it all back together again. **3. Be able to play it 3 times in a row correctly!**	1. Go over all of the notes again. 2. Focus on any key signatures, accidentals or other notes or fingerings you don't understand or forgot. **3. Be able to play it 3 times in a row correctly!**	1. Go through the notes and rests one at a time, slowly. 2. Make sure you understand all of the notes and fingerings. **3. Be able to play it 3 times in a row correctly!**

❏ Key signature: _____

❏ Focus on partials (how high/low you are playing); listen carefully & buzz your mouthpiece!

❏ Practice this slowly, maybe in "4+1" groups, tonguing the notes, then gradually speed up

❏ Rhythm: _____

❏ Articulation:

_____

❏ Your tone is fuzzy; the cause could be a leaky spit valve or pad, bad reed or mouthpiece, or embouchure; see me

❏ Play with more full sound & confidence!

❏ Your sound will improve if you use more air

Other Next Steps:

and assessment where they will have the greatest impact, teachers can teach all students the parts to one or a few small-group pieces. Then, when students are in their small groups, they are more free to focus on timing, tuning, and the like. Example 7.5 is a form for assessment of chamber ensembles.

Example 7.5: Chamber music critique
Adapted from Matt Temple

		This went well today	This is developing	This hindered your performance today
Chamber Music Critique				
Group members: _____				
Piece: _____				
UNITY OF SOUND				
How did individual and group <u>tone</u>, <u>blend</u>, <u>tuning</u>, and <u>balance</u> help or hinder the musical product?				
STAYING TOGETHER				
How did the group establish and maintain a single <u>ensemble tempo</u> and successfully negotiate <u>starting</u>, <u>stopping</u>, <u>transitions</u>, and <u>fermatas</u>?				
STYLE and EXPRESSIVITY				
How did individuals and the group use <u>stylistic</u> and <u>expressive musical elements</u> to communicate a clear and consistent musical message?				
ACCURACY				
How did individual and group <u>note accuracy</u>, <u>rhythmic accuracy</u>, and <u>technical fluency</u> help or hinder the musical product?				

Based on your ratings above, please describe in detail <u>one</u> area of strength:

Please describe in detail <u>one</u> area for further improvement:

Example 7.6: Chamber music evaluation

Chamber Music Evaluation			
Group Members: _____			
Piece: _____			
Evaluator: _____			
	Always	Usually	Sometimes

A
- CORRECT NOTES: *(Sounds good!)* — _____ _____ _____
- UNIFIED ARTICULATION: *(Note lengths match)* *(Heavy vs. light tongue)* — _____ _____ _____

B
- CORRECT RHYTHMS: *(Sounds good!)* — _____ _____ _____
- PLAYING TOGETHER: *(Starting & stopping)* *(Consistent tempo)* — _____ _____ _____

C
- CLEAR BALANCE: *(All parts same volume)* *(Melody always easy to hear)* — _____ _____ _____
- PURE BLEND & TUNING: *(Good, blended sounds)* *(Matching pitch)* — _____ _____ _____

D
- ARTFUL MUSICIANSHIP: *(Dynamic contrast)* *(Phrasing/direction of the line)* — _____ _____ _____
- PROFESSIONALISM: *(Confidence)* *(Stage presence/behavior)* — _____ _____ _____

The questions at the bottom encourage the evaluator to focus his or her comments. Example 7.6 is another chamber music evaluation. The criteria are broken into four groups to facilitate "jigsaw" peer assessment; students focus their listening on one area (e.g., letter B is their "piece of the puzzle"). Both examples use clarifying language to help performers and assessors.

INFORMAL SELF AND PEER ASSESSMENT

An underappreciated difference between collegiate or professional musicians and student musicians is the degree to which they are aware of their own contributions to the performance and how their parts relate to the others. These abilities are learned just like any other. Because students and not the teacher will actually be making the music onstage, involving them in performance assessment is a key ingredient of building these abilities and thus a high-functioning ensemble.

Student feedback is dependent on the quality of the insights underpinning it. For each rehearsal instruction, teachers can communicate to the students how success will be evaluated by saying "We'll know we've got it when . . ." or "We can move on when we hear . . ." This way of showing students the target enables students not only to hit it but to assess whether they or their peers have as well. For example:

> Let's have just the strings go back to measure 13 and we'll all listen to whether the cello/bass melody is easy to hear over the violin accompaniment. Violins, remember that if you can't hear the melody on the stage, the audience can't hear it either. We'll move on when we can clearly hear the melody. Instruments up . . . OK, winds, could you hear the melody that time? Thumbs up, down, or sideways. Violins, what about you?

Box 7.4: SIX BENEFITS OF STUDENT INVOLVEMENT WITH ASSESSMENT IN REHEARSALS

1. It cultivates students' critical listening and evaluation skills, which can improve their ability to self-monitor and self-correct in current practice sessions and future musical endeavors.
2. It conveys ownership of the performance.
3. It relieves the teacher of always delivering the bad news.
4. It gives credibility to the feedback, as students nearly always believe a large group of peers, and feedback offered by peers may be phrased in a way that is understandable.
5. It holds students' attention during a time when it might wander.
6. It engages students and reduces performance pressure.

One of the advantages self and peer assessment can bring to an ensemble is the opportunity for varied student groupings. Strategically shifting who is performing and who is evaluating gives students new opportunities for listening and evaluation, and also keeps the process novel. Groupings could be:

- By section (high strings/low strings; sopranos/altos)
- By textural function (melody, countermelody, accompaniment, etc. as the score dictates)
- By age or year in school
- By seating (sections, rows, or alternating As and Bs sitting next to one another)
- By playful attributes (toothpaste color, people who traveled for Labor Day, etc.)

QFATs in the rehearsal

QFATs are easy to implement, keep the class moving, and promote non-judgmental but meaningful interaction between teacher and students, and especially among students themselves. Many teachers wish that the students would exhibit more leadership or ownership. What they might mean is that they wish students would give feedback to others about their performance and their attitudes and proactively practice parts as needed.

Box 7.5: QUICK SELF AND PEER ASSESSMENT STRATEGIES FOR REHEARSALS

- Any QFATs from Chapter 3
- Point to the section that . . .
- Tell your neighbor (or section) one thing that you will do differently next time.
- Yesterday's News: tell your neighbor what you remember from yesterday's class, and what a focus of today should be.
- Use classroom whiteboards to report key measure numbers or concepts.
- The Sphinx: each student must tell the teacher two things she or he will improve today (or say two features of a key concept such as legato style) in order to gain entry to the room
- Adapt the Skills strategies from Chapter 6
- Use technology to implement any of these strategies

Self and peer assessment cultivate leadership skills by providing students with the tools to speak to each other in specific, affirmative, and honest ways. They cultivate ownership by providing them with tools for diagnosis and remediation of errors in their performance as well as Dispositions and work habits.

An advantage of such QFATs as "Fist to Five" or "Yesterday's News" is that students can easily become accustomed to using them, and the teacher is freed from constantly explaining new procedures. A few examples of implementing these strategies in a rehearsal might be:

- Violins and violas play the F scale while cellos and basses rate the tuning on only the B♭ as thumbs up, sideways, or down. Try again, then switch.
- Altos sing the passage while sopranos follow along in their music and put a breath mark by any place where everyone took a breath at the same time. Share and try again, then switch.
- Divide students into pairs. The first person plays the chromatic scale and the second person says "Oh, snap!" if he or she hears a wrong note. Share any missed fingerings and try again, then switch.
- Half the class performs a crescendo while the other half uses their hands to show the amount of dynamic contrast they heard. Share and try again, then switch.
- The rest of the band chants the beat division while the bass line and associated percussion play; then chanters share any places where the tempo changed, then progressively move each part of the texture from chanting to playing.

Teachers can also invite a single student or a panel of students to come to the front of the room and listen to the ensemble. Students nearly always find this enjoyable and revelatory. The teacher may conduct, students may try their hands at conducting, or the ensemble may have no conductor. Students also find it entertaining if the teacher trades places with one of them, handing over the baton in exchange for a cello or folder. Since students need scaffolding to engage in productive at-home practice, using rehearsals to model error detection and problem-solving strategies may accomplish two goals: fixing the issue at hand for today and "teaching students to fish" on their own for tomorrow.[4]

Technology also allows this process to be interactive, engaging, and instantaneous. Many platforms can be configured to allow students to quickly share feedback with their peers. If the classroom has a projector, it can display student responses with live tallies like TV talent show voting.

Students can also suggest or vote on focus areas for home practice or tomorrow's rehearsal at the end of class.

Terminology

Terminology is a frequently overlooked enabling skill of PPA. If the focus of a lesson is developing listening and evaluation skills, teachers may wish to use plain English in their questioning and accept student responses in plain English. If the focus of the lesson is terminology, the teacher may select excerpts—from the group's own performance or rehearsal recordings—that illustrate positive and negative (even humorously so) examples of diction, balance, tempo, and so on. If terminology is not the focus of the lesson, teachers may provide suggested feedback to student assessors, such as "sentence starters" or checkbox comments. It is a tall order to address terminology, evaluation skills, and performance skills in a single lesson with inexperienced musicians. Students can have a terminology lesson another day.

FORMAL SELF AND PEER ASSESSMENT

Listening Logs

Perhaps the most basic type of formal PPA is student self evaluation. It can be overwhelming for students to listen to a complete performance of a piece and come up with intelligent comments. "Throwing students into the deep end" with a recording of an entire piece and a judge's sheet may not yield useful results. Especially at the outset, teachers may choose to narrow their students' focus, as in Example 7.7. It is also desirable for teachers to

Example 7.7: Student self evaluation

Rehearsal letter	How *musically* I played my part			How *accurately* I played my part			Questions I have for Mr. Roberts	My Next Steps for this section
Beginning–A	☺	😐	☹	☺	😐	☹		
A–B	☺	😐	☹	☺	😐	☹		
B–1st ending	☺	😐	☹	☺	😐	☹		

allow students to *just listen to the music* and see what they notice and appreciate. I certainly do not bring a paper rubric to the symphony.

When directed listening is desirable, teachers often turn to Listening Logs to help guide students through the process. Focused questions, possibly with answer choices provided, are scaffolding for less experienced evaluators, such as Examples 7.8 and 7.9. More advanced Logs might contain focused but more open-ended questions such as in Examples 7.10 and 7.11. Teachers could also establish a focus for listening by asking one question or just a few at a time, focused on one musical concept each (Example 7.12).

Example 7.8: Listening Log with yes/no questions

1. Could you hear an obvious crescendo before letter C?
_____ YES _____ NO _____ UNSURE *I'm unsure because:*
2. Could you clearly hear both of the soloists at the end?
_____ YES _____ NO _____ UNSURE *I'm unsure because:*
3. Did the tempo stay steady at the repeat?
_____ YES _____ NO _____ UNSURE *I'm unsure because:*

Example 7.9: Listening Log with closed-ended questions

1. Did we stay together better the first time or the second time?
_____ First time _____ Second time
2. How many wrong notes did you hear from measures 1–11?
_____ 0 _____ 1–2 _____ 3 or more
3. What happened to the tempo in the chorus?
_____ Slowed down _____ Sped up _____ Stayed the same
4. Vote for a place to work on diction:
_____ First verse _____ Second verse _____ Chorus
5. Which part was louder at the beginning?
_____ Tenor/Bass _____ Soprano/Alto _____ About the same
6. Where do we have the best dynamic contrast?
_____ First verse _____ Second verse _____ Chorus
7. Anything else you noticed? *(Please be helpful and respectful with your comments.)*

Example 7.10: Listening Log with open-ended questions

1. What was the place we made the biggest dynamic contrast?

2. Is there a section you think is too loud or too soft at the trio, or do we have good balance?

3. Were there any words you couldn't understand?

4. Write down any places where we all took a breath at the same time.

Example 7.11: Rehearsal progress Listening Log

1. If you were the director for a day, what would you rehearse and why?

2. What improvements have we made since the last time you listened?

3. If you had to assign yourself <u>one</u> thing to practice before the dress rehearsal, what would it be? What practice strategies would be most effective?

4. Which verses do <u>you</u> need to memorize before the concert? What are some good ways to work on memorization of text outside of class?

5. Are there any situations where you think a particular section might not understand how their part sounds to the rest of the group? Write a positive suggestion to another section that's phrased in a way that makes them feel good about receiving it.

Example 7.12: Listening Log by concept

(Diction) What are some places that you noticed the text was especially easy to understand?

(Diction) What are some words that an audience might have trouble understanding?

(Dynamics) Were there any places where you noticed that we were especially loud or soft?

(Dynamics) Were there any places where you noticed that we didn't really change volume when you thought we would?

(Balance) What are some spots where you thought that we did a great job making sure that both parts sounded equal to each other?

(Balance) What are some spots where you thought that either the sopranos or the altos were too loud or soft in relation to one another, or where you couldn't hear what you wanted to hear?

To address multiple concepts, the teacher could play a recording several times, once per question, so that students have a discrete focus each time they listen. Alternatively, the teacher could employ the jigsaw approach; together, the class constructs the complete picture, confronted with the interdependence of their assigned musical elements. This usually leads to productive discussion about what group and individual Next Steps should be. A further option is to edit the recording so students listen to excerpts rather than an entire piece. This conserves both class time and student attention, and it can be done quickly using basic software.

A variation on the Listening Log is the Anticipation Guide.[5] Students answer each evaluation question twice. The first time is before they hear the recording; the students predict or "anticipate" what the answer will be. The students' minds and ears then have clear goals for the second listening, which will either confirm or deny their predictions. Listening Logs can be used with professional recordings as well, helping students to know "where they are going." Example 7.13 is a Listening Log type of Anticipation Guide, while Example 7.14 is a variation for use during the course of a rehearsal.

Teachers can post rehearsal recordings online, enabling most students to listen outside of class time. Some websites allow students to comment on a particular moment in the recording; students could be assigned to provide (for example) two positive and two constructive comments. A portfolio

Example 7.13: Anticipation Guide for listening

BEFORE YOU LISTEN	Yep!	Maybe	Nope
1. Overall, do you think this piece is ready for the concert?	_____	_____	_____
2. Do you expect to hear dynamic contrast at the end?	_____	_____	_____
3. Do you think we stayed together during the accelerando?	_____	_____	_____
4. Write one more thing you expect to hear on the recording:			

AFTER YOU LISTEN	Yep!	Maybe	Nope
1. Now, do you think this piece is ready for the concert?	_____	_____	_____
2. Did you hear dynamic contrast at the end?	_____	_____	_____
3. Did we stay together during the accelerando?	_____	_____	_____
4. Did you hear what you expected? Please give specifics.			
My or our Next Steps:			

Example 7.14: Anticipation Guide for rehearsing

BEFORE THE RUN-THROUGH

Agree   Disagree

_____   _____   1. I feel comfortable maintaining my part between letter B and letter C.
_____   _____   2. I can easily remember <u>all</u> of the text.
_____   _____   3. I feel comfortable with the step-touch movement at the end.

AFTER THE RUN-THROUGH

Agree   Disagree

_____   _____   1. I felt comfortable maintaining my part between letter B and letter C.
_____   _____   2. I could easily remember <u>all</u> of the text.
_____   _____   3. I felt comfortable with the step-touch movement at the end.

My Next Steps:

---

consisting of a series of these would be a remarkable artifact. Students can also complete a paper or electronic Listening Log or Anticipation Guide at home, possibly with individual focus areas that can be assembled like a jigsaw at school. Easy recording and distribution of video recordings is also possible, although teachers must comply with district policies regarding video recording and release. Students can be distracted from critical listening by looking at themselves or their friends, but video can help students understand how audiences experience their performances.

Road Maps

One tool I have found particularly effective for self-PPA is a Road Map, such as Example 7.15. Road Maps are tools to help students track their progress toward learning their parts. At the beginning of the rehearsal process, then at regular intervals (e.g., every Friday), students play each section, stopping in between to record a self assessment. This provides each student with an individualized graphical representation of what to practice at home, take to a private lesson, or emphasize during class. The presence of a Road Map in

Example 7.15: Road Map

Pas Redoublé Road Map To Awesome						
Beginner:	I am in the beginning stages					
Apprentice:	I can play most of the notes/rhythms					
Master:	I can play nearly all of the notes/rhythms *and* I am starting to get the style & tempo					
Grand Master:	I have mastered the part *and* I am comfortable with the style & tempo					
Legend:	I have mastered the part, style and tempo *and* I am making art with my playing (or, I *tacet*)					

	Never played it	Beginner	Apprentice	Master	Grand Master	Legend
1–6						
7–21						
22–37						
38–53						
54–62						
...						
217–End						

students' folders may also facilitate individual practice, either before class or simultaneously during class. As a Road Map is an application of the Listening Log concept, it is usable in all of the ways outlined in the previous paragraphs.

OFF-THE-PODIUM PPA CONSIDERATIONS

The quality of a rehearsal recording is not critical. A simple recording with the built-in microphone in a computer, or even a mobile device, will suffice in most situations. The biggest challenge is often finding a microphone placement that will offer a reasonable picture of balance.[6] Teachers interested in classroom recording equipment might be wise to prioritize ease of use with editing software over sound fidelity. If the biggest problem on the recording is the microphones, things are going well! Self and peer assessment are not the only ways to use recordings for PPA. Many teachers make a rehearsal recording at regular intervals (e.g., every Friday) and use it to provide students with observations, reminders, and new targets.

Dispositions such as attitudes, preferences, and self-efficacy change from piece to piece and from concert to concert. As Dispositions affect student behavior and work habits, it is sensible for the teacher to possess assessment information about them. The following example is no substitute for teachers' interpersonal awareness of students' sentiments, but

Example 7.16: Repertoire disposition assessment

Our concert pieces:	Rainier Sunrise	Journey	Quartz Mountain Blues
How much do you like listening to piece?	0 1 2 3 4 5	0 1 2 3 4 5	0 1 2 3 4 5
How much do you like playing this piece?	0 1 2 3 4 5	0 1 2 3 4 5	0 1 2 3 4 5
Why?			
How well can you play this piece today?	0 1 2 3 4 5	0 1 2 3 4 5	0 1 2 3 4 5
How well do you expect us to play this piece at the concert?	0 1 2 3 4 5	0 1 2 3 4 5	0 1 2 3 4 5
How much have you practiced this piece outside of class?	0 1 2 3 4 5	0 1 2 3 4 5	0 1 2 3 4 5

students who are given a space for anonymous expression may well be inclined to be more honest. Even when they are uncomfortable for us, we need to know our students' truths.

SUMMARY

Assessment and feedback strategies can be effective tools for performance preparation. Performance preparation assessment can take place on or off of the podium; in the moment or planned in advance. Assessment practices in the rehearsal, whether led by the teacher, peers, or individuals themselves, can guide students to increased understanding, performance ability, ownership, and confidence.

TERMS

- Performance preparation assessment
- Rehearsal
- Rehearsal frame

ACTIVITIES

7.1. List and describe several potential differences between a Maestro rehearsal and assessment-focused teaching from the podium.

7.2. Make a table or Venn diagram with two categories: "Off the podium" and "On the podium." List which outcomes might be most appropriate for each.

7.3. Review a video of you or someone else teaching a school ensemble. Diagram the lesson in terms of rehearsal frames. Did most frames follow the sequence in Figure 7.1? What else do you notice?

7.4. Think about feedback that you have frequently given or received in rehearsals. Choose one enabling skill underlying the feedback you have received. Craft learning targets and possible assessments (using KRSPD) for this enabling skill.

SECTION THREE
Grades

CHAPTER 8

Grading Basics

Grading, reporting and communicating student learning are [among] educators' greatest responsibilities. . . . Yet despite the importance of these activities, few teachers have any formal training on grading or reporting. . . . As a result, even educators dissatisfied with their present systems lack direction in their efforts to make changes.

Jane Bailey and Jay McTighe[1]

Box 8.1: CHAPTER 8 ESSENTIAL QUESTIONS

1. What do grades mean, and how are they used?
2. Why are some aspects of traditional grading problematic for students?
3. How can grades be structured to facilitate the learning process?

This quote is over twenty years old, and it is just as relevant today. Grading is an emotionally charged but widely misunderstood endeavor for students, parents, and teachers. Many teachers, schools, and districts have recently sought to clarify and improve their grading philosophies and practices, while others have considered whether to eliminate grades altogether. Still, grading remains a central task for most educators. A succinct definition of grades comes from Guskey and Jung: "In education, **grades** are the symbols, words, or numerals that teachers assign to evidence of student learning to signify different levels of achievement."[2] Therefore, the process of **grading** involves someone, typically the teacher, assigning a grade (or **mark** in some countries) to a student's achievement or learning. Grades are intended to function as a communication tool. Unfortunately, the message is often lost. This chapter will explore grades and grading in general. Chapter 9 extends and applies these principles to music courses.

THE USES OF GRADES

The most obvious use of grades is reporting student achievement or learning. Grades are the most common measuring stick for "how school is going." Parents may use information from a report card in a variety of child-rearing decisions, from time use to tutoring to career plans. School personnel also use grade reports in a variety of ways, such as course placements, academic interventions, and graduation. Grade reports also have ramifications well into adulthood, with employment opportunities, university admissions, and scholarship dollars at stake. Although they have myriad uses today, the inescapable original intent behind grades was to sort and rank students.[3] Even though colleges and employers surely appreciate ready-made rankings, the question of how this helps the students themselves is rarely asked.

Adults often leverage the significance we attach to grades in an attempt to influence or control students' behavior. Societal norms have led to the understanding that higher grades are "good" grades and lower grades are "bad" grades. Teachers commonly expect that a "bad" grade will be a motivator for a student. Schools may recognize students on the honor roll or otherwise celebrate those who get good grades, and they may also use grades for negative reinforcement, such as withdrawing eligibility for sports teams or prom tickets. Schools and teachers may also use grades to reward desirable behaviors such as participating in fundraisers or parents volunteering with the boosters, or to punish students for undesirable behaviors such as talking, not turning in homework, forgetting supplies, or missing school.

PROBLEMS WITH GRADES
The single letter grade

Even though the A–F scale has been around for approximately a hundred years, there has never been widespread agreement about what it means.[4] Using a single letter or numerical score to represent a student's "overall" performance in a class conflates many disparate pieces of information. Basic questions such as those in Box 8.2 are often left unanswered by schools and teachers or misunderstood by students and families.

- Are grades norm-referenced (judged against peers), criterion-referenced (judged against a pre-defined standard), or growth-referenced (judged against self)?
- Does the grade reflect meeting academic standards? Effort? Improvement? Citizenship?
- Does the grade reflect a student's work in this class, or is it a reflection of the skills, experiences, and orientations with which the student began the class?
- Do grades distinguish between students who can't do the work and students who won't do the work?
- Does an A signal that the student is exceptional, or just that the student met the standard? What do the other letters mean?
- Do grades mean the same thing in all classrooms in all schools?

If the primary goal is communication, the use of a single grade is problematic. If it ostensibly represents everything, it truly represents nothing. As grading expert Ken put it: "To serve so many different purposes, one letter or number symbol must carry many types of information (achievement, effort, behavior, etc.) in the grade. Putting together such a variety of information makes it very difficult to clearly understand what grades mean."[5] Furthermore, even if the teacher or school has clearly defined criteria for assigning grades, it is no sure thing that students, families, or others will interpret the grades in the way that the school intended. Too often, when asked why they got a particular grade, students honestly reply, "I don't know!" Sometimes, not even the teacher can say for sure, deferring to a calculation from grade formulas or software. Something is wrong here!

Objectivity

Grades have an air of truth and objectivity. This belies the fact that all grades are, to a healthy extent, arbitrary. Grades are normally based on assessments, which readers of this book know are never entirely objective. In addition, the result of varying policies and calculations is that the same student performance is graded differently by different teachers. Many unquestioned but entrenched grading conventions exist, such as those in Box 8.3.

- . . . a B is 79.5 percent–89.4 percent?
- . . . the fourth quarter of the school year counts as much as the first quarter?
- . . . senior year counts as much as freshman year when figuring GPA?
- . . . a student who didn't complete homework assignments but did well on tests should be regarded the same was as a student who did the homework but couldn't pass the tests?
- . . . 61 percent is sufficient for promotion or graduation, but 59 percent is not?
- . . . a student who learned the material after everyone else should be penalized?
- . . . a late paper would get full credit up to twenty-four hours late and half credit one to six days late and would be meaningless more than a week late, even if it was beautifully written?

Few teachers can say where their grading policies originated. Still, these and other conventions play at least as much of a role in students' grades as student performance. More factors are in Box 8.4. Grades' questionable "objectivity" is unfortunate, given their lasting consequences for students.

Grades and learning

In addition to being ineffective communicators, traditional grades are not educational. Previous chapters outline aspects of Assessment for Learning: targeting specific skills or behaviors, encouraging continued effort, clearly communicating what's working, and offering specific action steps for improvement. Grading, which is quantitative and not descriptive feedback, does none of those things. As McTighe and O'Connor wrote: "Too many educators consider scores as feedback when, in fact, they fail the specificity test. Pinning a letter (B–) or a number (82%) on a student's work is no more helpful than 'nice job' or 'you can do better.'"[6] It would be possible to have fertile learning environments with no grades at all. Learning does not require value judgments.

In addition to being unnecessary for learning, grades can actually be counterproductive. While the threat of a grade penalty may send high-achieving students scrambling, grades tend to be ineffective motivators for students who haven't fared as well. Children who are used to getting

Some elements of a grade seem obvious:
- Tests and quizzes
- Projects
- Homework and classwork

But, there is much more lurking beneath the surface:
- Teacher and school philosophies and policies
- What's in the curriculum
- Which elements of the curriculum a teacher chooses to emphasize
- What's on the test or other assessments
- Instructional time
- Teacher competency
- Teachers' personal definitions of "participation" and "responsibility" and how these are affected by attitudes toward students' socioeconomic status, gender and gender expression, ethnicity, exceptionality, and other characteristics
- Teachers' attitudes toward individual students
- The extent to which teachers are invested, thorough, and careful while grading
- Student and family resources and circumstances
- Luck

"bad" grades or have low self-efficacy are unlikely to be persuaded by the threat of yet another negative report. As Guskey and Jung put it: "No research supports the idea that low grades prompt students to try harder. More often, low grades lead students to withdraw from learning. To protect their self-images, many students regard the low grade as irrelevant or meaningless. Others may blame themselves for the low grade but feel helpless to improve."[7] This helplessness is compounded by situations that are out of students' control, such as not being able to afford instrument repairs or being directed by working parents to miss school to take care of younger siblings who are sick. Grades further embody extrinsic motivation, engendering performance goals (fixed mindset) rather than learning goals (growth mindset).[8] This fixed mindset can be particularly toxic for students who already feel stigmatized or insecure about academic struggles, too often leading to the outcomes Guskey and Jung described. School leaders, parents, teachers, and even students are frequently unaware aware of these dynamics.

> ### Box 8.5: WHAT'S NECESSARY FOR LEARNING?
>
> Children can learn without:
> - Summative assessment
> - Grades
> - Deadlines
> - Comparison to peers
> - Judgment
> - "I told you so" or "Maybe this isn't for you"
>
> Children cannot learn without:
> - Formative assessment
> - Descriptive feedback
> - Successive attempts
> - Comparison to standards
> - Encouragement
> - Hope

The use of grades as a punishment for misbehavior or "irresponsibility" is also of serious concern. Judgments about behavior are inherently arbitrary, impossible to apply uniformly, and subject to each teacher's personal biases and stereotypes. Grades designed to be punitive are not educational. Veteran teachers know that a grade penalty rarely results in lasting change to students' behaviors and attitudes. In addition, school discipline policies usually mean that grade punishments represent double jeopardy for students. Rick Wormeli emphasized that "we are teaching adults-in-the-making, not adults."[9] Gandhi affirmed, "Forgiveness is an attribute of the strong."

GRADES THAT FACILITATE LEARNING

All of this means that our current grading policies confer a systemic advantage on students who are positioned to get good grades or are accustomed to getting them and a disadvantage on students who aren't so lucky or who have received poor grades in the past. If the purpose of education is merely to let students "sink or swim" on their own and report to colleges and employers who sank and who swam, then this system is fine. However, if the purpose of education is to give a swimming lesson to those who need one, then traditional grading practices are ripe for reconsideration.

School as a "learning game"

Students often have two paths to a good grade. One is to learn a lot and master course content. Alternatively, they can demonstrate compliance and obedience, do homework on time, "participate" during class, and so on. Students often come to view the purpose of school to be grades, not learning; points, not progress. As noted in Chapter 1, evaluation methods can change the nature of school tasks. The anticipation of the high-stakes grade often results in students avoiding risks and divergent thinking.[10] Instead, students may prefer to play it safe by attempting to complete tasks and conduct themselves in ways that seem more likely to please the teacher, rather than ways that maximize growth or reflect personal choice. This is not what most educators want. As Ken O'Connor says, "Everyone involved must see school as a *learning* game, not a *grading* game."[11]

The majority of students would like to learn a lot *and* have good grades. However, students face more pressure to get good grades than to master content, grow as a person, be inquisitive, and discover what makes them happy. If the only route to the honor roll involves understanding, completeness, original thought, and exemplary performance, those are the things that students playing either game will do. Students only play the grading game when school allows or encourages them to.

Standards-based grading

An alternative to traditional percentage grading that has traditionally been used in elementary schools but has begun to gain wider acceptance at the secondary level is **standards-based grading** (SBG).[12] The premise of SBG is that students' grades are based only on the extent to which they have mastered the most important and enduring curricular goals or content standards (sometimes called **power standards**)—not the grading game. Performance on each standard is reported separately from the others. As an analogy, if someone taking a driver's test gets a 100 percent on the written portion and 60 percent on the driving portion, it would seem to be poor policy to issue a license on the basis of an acceptable average of 80 percent. SBG philosophy holds that this driver didn't actually get 80 percent on anything. The written and driving scores reflect different competencies, and while an average is mathematically possible, it is logically invalid.

Central to the philosophy of standards-based grading is the idea that grades are decisions teachers make using their professional judgment instead of The Math of traditional percentage grading. Any student who has been told, "In my opinion, you did A work, but your score worked out to be an 88 percent, so you got a B+ and there's nothing I can do about that" understands the absurdity of letting a five-dollar calculator (or grading software that performs essentially the same functions as a five-dollar calculator) have more of a say in evaluating their performance than a licensed, experienced professional educator. While scores (e.g., number of correct items on a written test) provide useful information about student performance, there is a crucial difference between data (scores) and the interpretation of that data (grades). Some teachers prefer the veneer of objectivity associated with The Math, but grade objectivity is illusory. Teachers cannot be helpless bystanders in the grading process. Computers can't assign grades, and grades can't assign themselves. A professional educator's best evaluation of a student's performance, taking all available information into account, is more valid than any mathematical formula.

Levels and labels

One common critique of the A–F system is that there are too many possibilities (thirteen between A+ and F). There is wide agreement that a smaller number of levels is optimal. Having too many levels reduces the accuracy and consistency of the grades. Who can meaningfully (or "objectively") discriminate between a "C paper" and a "C– paper", and how does that distinction help students? As noted in Chapter 4, three or four levels may be ideal. The A–F grading system is so firmly entrenched in people's minds that, to successfully implement standards-based grading, it may be necessary to use entirely different language to describe student performance. Letters and numbers on ten- or hundred-point scales evoke traditional grade interpretation.

Standards-based grades are criterion-referenced (student performance is judged against a fixed standard of achievement) rather than norm-referenced (performance is judged against peers). If everyone in the class meets the standard, then everyone's grade reflects meeting the standard. If teachers intend to use criterion-referenced (or construct-referenced) evaluation, it is also essential to use criterion-referenced grade labels. The rubric descriptors in Table 4.1 work nicely as grade labels, since SBG is in essence using a holistic rubric for each curricular goal or power standard.

THREE PRINCIPLES FOR DETERMINING GRADES

School districts often mandate how grades are reported. However, principles of SBG translate to any system.

Box 8.6: THREE PRINCIPLES FOR DETERMINING GRADES

1. Grades should include information on student achievement.
2. Grades should exclude everything that's not student achievement.
3. Grades should reflect where students ended up, not where they started.

Grades should include student achievement

This is the simplest of the three principles to implement. Teachers are responsible for ensuring that grades accurately reflect student achievement by using multiple assessments to acquire enough information to make a judgment about each student's mastery of goal or power standard. Too narrow a view of what constitutes "academic achievement" often means that only certain elements of a curriculum are graded—and, by extension, valued.[13] One of the useful features of the KRSPD framework is its ability to help teachers recognize that "achievement" goes far beyond part performance and written tests. A single assessment frequently involves more than one standard. The grades for each standard should be recorded separately, just like the driver's test. "You got a B on the final exam" is not nearly as informative as "Your theory skills are strong; where you can improve is your singing tone."

Grades should exclude everything that's not student achievement

Teachers understandably want to communicate non-academic information about students. Work habits and citizenship are often among the most important outcomes of school. Still, their inclusion in a letter grade muddies its communication. The solution is to report non-academic information separately. If the school does not provide a mechanism for separate reporting, the teacher can easily devise one in order to preserve clarity in the official grade.

Penalties for late or missed work are a common way that non-academic information ends up in grades. (Other non-academic grade influences specific to music are included in Chapter 9.) Teachers often have a strong feeling that there must be a consequence if something is not submitted on time. However, children turn things in late and don't do things for all sorts of reasons, including lack of confidence, health problems, family circumstances, and pressure (from the school!) to be involved in extracurricular activities. We educators certainly forgive ourselves for occasionally having an "off day" or needing to prioritize commitments. Students who turn in a few assignments late may only need reminders, or they may need no action from the school at all. Students who habitually miss assignments or turn them in late may merit intervention by pupil support staff, but there are more effective options than grade penalties, which neither investigate nor solve root causes. Late-work penalties do not teach "responsibility," but they do have the effect of discouraging students from completing schoolwork. This is not a desirable outcome. Student work should be evaluated according to its quality, regardless of when it arrives at the teacher's desk.

Many teachers have a singular (if unstated) attachment to the idea that students must complete every task that the teacher has assigned, without exception. Accordingly, there are often stiff grade penalties when work is not completed, usually a grade of zero. Similar to penalties for late work, the zero is a distortion of the grade as a report of academic achievement. This doesn't mean that student follow-through isn't important—it certainly is—but it does highlight that turning things in is not the same as academic achievement. In addition, assigning a zero that cannot be made up relieves the student from the responsibility of having to do the work, sending the message that it wasn't that important in the first place.

Work that has not been completed can be recorded as "Missing" or "Incomplete" instead. The teacher can follow up with students and families until the assignment is complete and can be properly evaluated. Teachers who insist on penalties for missing work might consider entering a grade of 50 percent instead of zero. The zero has an outsized effect on averaged grades that are figured on a 0–100 scale; it is not just an F, but an F-----. A grade of 50 percent isn't "giving students something for nothing." It's still an F, just a more mathematically sensible one. In all cases, even when using the zero, the grade must be recoverable; the emphasis is on getting the student to complete the work. This is not the same as fail-proofing the class, or letting kids off the hook. There certainly is a time, such as the end of a term, when teachers have to make a judgment about whether students achieved mastery of course content and report grades accordingly.[14] However, students deserve every opportunity to recover from their mistakes and show what they have learned.

Teachers justifiably want students to follow assignment directions and present their work professionally. When these non-academic considerations are graded, assignment grades are confounded. Students who follow the directions have their grades inflated relative to their academic performance, and students who didn't follow the directions have their grades correspondingly lowered. Instead of including these considerations in a summative evaluation, teachers can instead establish them as **gateway criteria**. If a gateway criterion is not met, the work is returned to the student as incomplete rather than unsatisfactory. It is then the student's responsibility to submit a complete product for evaluation of the content mastery it represents. Assess the process; grade the product.

Grades should reflect where students ended up, not where they started

Traditionally, a grade represents the student's achievement over the course of a reporting period—that is, the extent to which the student mastered the content by the time the term ended. In traditional grading, what happens early in the semester and what happens at the end of the semester have the same effect on the final grade. A student who earns a low grade based on early performance but turns it around—what the school encouraged him to do—may be rewarded with a maximum final grade of C. This is a strong disincentive to try to catch up.

In order for grades to be an accurate report of student performance, students should be allowed to receive full credit if they demonstrate mastery of the course content after several attempts and after initial due dates. Learning does not always follow the teacher's calendar. In fact, redos and retakes represent persistence and merit praise instead of penalties. Teachers who didn't pass a licensure exam on the first try were allowed to retake the test and receive the same license as those who did. Why do we treat our students differently? Do teachers think that they would have learned "responsibility" if they weren't allowed to get a teaching license?

It is reasonable for teachers to take steps to not have second (and third) attempts, and late assignments, become burdensome. Retakes and reteaching may have to be scheduled at the teacher's convenience. There may be hard deadlines, such as one week before the end of the semester or before a concert. Teachers or schools may choose to attach some sort of non-punitive "opportunity cost" to retakes and redos; for example, retakes may have to be done at lunch. Perhaps a review activity or practice session with a section leader is required before a retake is allowed. However, having to do the same assignment multiple times may be enough of a cost by itself. Teachers may also wish to limit or prohibit perfectionist redos, like students with an A– trying to get an A. Over time, sensible policies will emerge that fit each teacher's situation.

For their grades to reflect where students finished and not where they started, teachers should assign less weight—or, ideally, no weight—to diagnostic and formative assessments. The purpose of summative assessment is to evaluate the extent to which students have mastered course objectives, which aligns with the purpose of grades. Formative assessments do not have the same function; they are for learning, not reporting. How a student performs on formative assessments should not affect the final grade any more than how a musician performs in early practice sessions affects the evaluation of her senior recital. Diagnostic and formative assessment can be recorded as "completed" in the gradebook or can include a score with a zero (or minuscule) weight, so that the final grade calculation only or predominantly includes summative assessments. In fact, formative assessment does not require grades, or any recording at all. Jan Chappuis and Judy Arter remind us to "assess a lot; grade a little."[15]

Assessments that happen later in the reporting period can be given more weight—possibly much more weight—than assessments that happen earlier. If the student doesn't demonstrate mastery of September's content until November, the final grade should still indicate that the content was mastered. Weighted grades can make early assessments have less impact on the grade than later assessments, which are often cumulative in nature. Teachers can also simply update a previous gradebook entry upon receipt of new information. As Ken O'Connor says, "Grade in pencil."[16]

FURTHER CONSIDERATIONS

Organizing the gradebook

It is helpful for teachers to organize their gradebooks by curricular elements (such as a section for "performing music" and a section for "reading music") rather than by assessment type (such as a section for "tests" and a section for "homework"). This reinforces the concept that school is a learning game ("Looks like I need to improve my work in 'Responding to Music'") rather than a grading game ("Looks like I need to do better on quizzes"). The KRSPD framework may also be useful for gradebook organization.

Separate categories for non-academic achievement such as work habits or citizenship are also invaluable.

Grade weights

Gradebooks that promote school as a learning game are weighted, rather than using "total points." Grades using **category weights** follow a formula such as 15 percent reading music; 45 percent performing music; 20 percent responding to music; 20 percent creating music, or a similar system aligned with the relative importance of learning goals or power standards for the course. Using **total points** (such as five points for each homework assignment, twenty points for a quiz, etc.) or weighting by assignment type (e.g., 10 percent homework, 25 percent participation, etc.) communicates to students that school is a series of hoops through which they have to jump, rather than ways in which they should grow and skills they should develop. Assigning non-academic categories a weight of zero allows easy communication with families without adversely affecting the final grade. Of course, this is only necessary when percentages are used.

Reporting formats

Teachers should feel free to supplement the traditional report card with materials that further explain grading procedures, the desired performance, the observed performance, and Next Steps for improvement, with any desired skills or non-academic goals. Office software with a mail-merge option can quickly generate such a document from a spreadsheet of student scores and comments. No matter how grades are reported, students and parents should always know what the current grade is, how it is determined, and what it means. Only grades that communicate understandable, current, and valid information are useful for learning.

SUMMARY

Even though grades are ever-present in education, they are seldom understood or thoughtfully determined. Grades can alter students' goals for and approaches to their schoolwork. For grades to function effectively as communication about student learning, they should exclude non-academic factors such as behavior and timeliness, prioritize summative assessment over formative assessment, and be determined by the teacher instead of mathematical formulas.

TERMS

- Grades
- Grading
- Marks
- Standards-based grading
- Power standard
- Gateway criteria
- Category weights
- Total points

ACTIVITIES

8.1. Recall a situation from your own experience as a student in which you felt that your grade did not match your performance. What causes or solutions from this chapter might be related to the situation?
8.2. Summarize how grading practices are related to fixed and growth mindsets. What recommendations would you make based on your summary?
8.3. Make a case for and against penalties for late and missed work.
8.4. Design a report card for your teaching area. What information might you, students, and families find helpful? How should it be formatted?

CHAPTER 9

Grading in the Ensemble Classroom

There is little consensus as to the best way to calculate overall grades in secondary music classes.

James Austin and Joshua Russell[1]

Box 9.1: CHAPTER 9 ESSENTIAL QUESTIONS

1. How have music grades traditionally been determined?
2. What can music teachers do to ensure that their grades are fair and educational?
3. How can educators navigate common controversies in music grading?

Few music educators regard grading as the best part of their jobs. Many treat grades as a nuisance paperwork task, more like purchase orders than a core educational responsibility. Others know their grading practices aren't perfect, but aren't quite sure how to fix them or don't think they have the time.[2] Still, grades remain consequential for students, families, administrators, colleges, and policymakers. If grades are to be given—and they are, in most cases, for the foreseeable future—then students and other stakeholders deserve grades that are well conceived.

Teachers are surprisingly wedded to their grading procedures. This is often due to grades' perceived function as extrinsic motivation for students to do things like practice their instruments or show up to rehearsals. However, as detailed in Chapter 8, this desire to control students can result in communication that is distorted and potential consequences that are lasting and unfair. In many ensemble classrooms, reconsidering grading practices involves moving away from "evidence of participation" and toward "evidence of learning."[3]

WHAT'S IN A MUSIC GRADE?

Many music ensemble grades are effectively determined by compliance with the teacher's behavior requirements: attendance, "effort" or "participation," turning in permission slips, and the like. However, even as these behaviors make the teacher's life easier, they are not indicative of students' musical understanding or ability. Content standards do not typically include black socks, signed handbook forms, or knowing when not to chew gum. These are important, but they can be emphasized by means other than grading. As noted in Chapter 8, teachers can and should track both academic and non-academic information. To ensure meaningfulness, the grade should include only academic data. Whether a student chews gum can be communicated separately. "Gum grades" are driven by what the *teacher* wants for an efficient program. Achievement grades are driven by the extent to which *students* hit their learning targets.

This is a paradigm shift for many music educators, but it is a worthwhile one. Behavior-focused grades are often determined by the amount of family support students are able to receive. Students whose families can deliver a forgotten folder, acquire the proper rosin or dress shoes, or know when a concert is happening and make transportation arrangements benefit in such a system. Furthermore, in a behavior-focused grading system, students are incentivized to prioritize participation over practicing, and attendance over achievement. This often leads to a disconnect between students' grades and their musical achievements. The best musicians—not the best rule followers—should have the best grades.

Other classes, particularly classes that are touted as rigorous, rarely employ behavior-driven grading systems. Parents, students, and administrators notice how grades are calculated. No one would accept gum grades in history or Spanish. If "what's measured is treasured," music teachers should carefully consider the values their gradebooks convey. "Gum grading" sends the message that music is a throwaway subject rather than the complex undertaking that music educators know it to be. Serious grading practices are important advocacy if music is to be regarded as a serious subject. However, in a 2010 survey, secondary ensemble teachers reported that their grades contained an average of 60 percent non-academic factors like attendance, attitude, and self-reported practice time.[4]

MEANINGFUL ENSEMBLE GRADES

Decisions underlying grade calculations

For music grades to reflect content mastery, music teachers need clarity about each decision that results in the final grade. The course objectives must be clear and include concrete definitions of mastery (Chapter 2). There must be multiple ways to gather information about student achievement and corresponding methods for processing the information to make judgments about the extent to which students have mastered each objective (Chapters 3–7). Finally, there must be a procedure to synthesize the various data points into an imperfect but sincere report about student achievement (Chapter 8). Put another way, in order for grades to serve their purpose, each link in the curriculum-to-grade chain in Figure 9.1 must be solid. If any link is weak or broken, the final grade is correspondingly invalid. It is unjust for students to receive poor grades from a flawed system.

Chapter 8 introduced the question of whether students are playing a "learning game" or a "grading game." Gradebooks organized to promote a grading game have categories such as homework, assignments, singing tests, participation, or attendance. The emphasis is on schooling routines. A gradebook promoting a learning game might include categories such as reading music, ensemble skills, singing technique, or "music in your life"— whatever the power standards or course goals might be. The emphasis is on learning and performance. One reason that music teachers resort to behavior-focused grading is that it is simpler than assessment of individual students' musical achievements. Hopefully, the strategies in this book have made valid student assessment feel attainable.

Deciding which assessments are included

Once non-academic factors have been excluded, the decision about comprises the grade is largely between fundamentals and repertoire. While part performance is central to ensemble classes, its inclusion in grades is

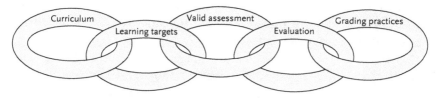

Figure 9.1: Links in the grading chain

awkward, especially when it is the primary basis. Even the most carefully designed concert program cannot be musically comprehensive, and PPA only encompasses a subset of Skill targets. Repertoire cannot be equally challenging for all students, or equally challenging across semesters or years, especially in instrumental ensembles where parts vary widely even within the same piece. This introduces confounders into grades, including the part the student happens to perform and the repertoire that happens to be chosen that term.

Each piece of repertoire requires enabling Knowledge, Reasoning, and Skills to perform. These enabling abilities range from being universally applicable to unique to a particular composition. Ensemble grades are most consistent, comprehensive, and equitable when they are based on the foundational Knowledge, Reasoning, and Skills that students need every concert or semester. Products can also be meaningfully included in grades when they are substantial elements of the curriculum. As it is often difficult to disaggregate individual contributions to a performance, any grades for repertoire should result from individual or small-group, rather than large-group, performance assessments before or after the concert.

Final grade determinations

Educators wishing to move away from traditional percentage measures toward a standards-based grading philosophy may wish to adopt a more holistic view of grading. Student achievement evidence can be categorized according to whatever level system the teacher uses. Reliability, one of the core components of grades, increases with fewer levels. The following examples use a three-level system of Proficient, Developing, and Beginning. (Chapter 8 contains an elaboration on level systems.) The teacher makes a judgment about each student's pattern of achievement with respect to each of the power standards, ideally based on multiple summative assessments of each. If student performance does not yield a clear answer about whether a standard has been met, further assessment is necessary. If a student hasn't completed all of the assessments but has clearly met the standard, further assessment is unnecessary. If the purpose of grades is reporting achievement, it is not mandatory for all students to have completed the same number of assessments by year's end.

Finally, the teacher converts the judgments about each standard into the grade reporting format specified by the school, as in Table 9.1. Tables 9.2 and 9.3 provide sample formulas for converting levels for standards into a single final grade. This removes pressure for students

Table 9.1: SAMPLE FINAL GRADES

Student	Music "power standards"				Music non-academic standards	
	Performing music	Reading music	Understanding music	Creating music	Letter grade	Being responsible	Being a good citizen
Brandon	Proficient	Proficient	Proficient	Developing	A	Always	Usually
Keisha	Proficient	Proficient	Beginning	Proficient	B	Usually	Always
Chris	Proficient	Developing	Developing	Proficient	B	Usually	Usually
Andrew	Developing	Proficient	Proficient	Proficient	A	Always	Area of Concern
Tiffany	Proficient	Beginning	Proficient	Proficient	B	Area of Concern	Always
Mateo	Proficient	Proficient	Proficient	Proficient	A	Always	Always

Table 9.2: SAMPLE FORMULA FOR STANDARDS-BASED
GRADES WITH FOUR POWER STANDARDS

Grades on the standards	Final grade (SBG format)	Final grade (letter format)
PPPP	Proficient	A
PPPD	Proficient	A
PPPB	Developing	B
PPDD	Proficient	B
PPDB	Developing	B
PPBB	Developing	B
PDDD	Developing	B
PDDB	Developing	B
PDBB	Developing	B
PBBB	Beginning	C
DDDD	Developing	C
DDDB	Developing	C
DDBB	Developing	C
DBBB	Beginning	D
BBBB	Beginning	F

Table 9.3: SAMPLE FORMULA FOR STANDARDS-BASED
GRADES WITH THREE POWER STANDARDS

Grades on the standards	Final grade (SBG format)	Final grade (letter format)
PPP	Proficient	A
PPD	Proficient	A
PPB	Developing	B
PDD	Developing	B
PDB	Developing	B
PBB	Developing	C
DDD	Developing	C
DDB	Developing	C
DBB	Beginning	D
BBB	Beginning	F

to argue over minuscule differences in "points" and instead focus on larger questions about mastery, areas for improvement, and Next Steps. Furthermore, it removes The Math from the decision-making process, freeing teachers to make sensible, sincere reports. Table 9.1 also includes reports on important non-academic factors. They use different level language (Always, Usually, or Area of Concern) to reinforce that they do not play a role in determining the students' grades. Although not included here, descriptions of grading procedures (including how grades are figured and what different levels represent) in syllabi, handbooks, and online gradebooks aid students and families with understanding their meaning. Detailed descriptions are assets to students, teachers, parents, and administrators. To avoid confusion, grade reports should either avoid or explain musical jargon.[5]

While this non-mathematical system is not weighted per se, teachers can make a power standard more or less determinative. A particularly salient power standard (such as performing) could have its own part of the grading decision tree, as in Table 9.4. A teacher wishing for certain power standards to play a smaller role in the final grade can combine two of them (e.g., in a four-standard system, combine two standards into one and use a three-standard system). In Table 9.4, a performing-centric grading system, a student who is a Beginning performer cannot earn an overall grade of Proficient, but a good performer who is Beginning with another standard can. These methods enable teachers to report grades fairly according to their own values and curricula.

Music teachers wishing or needing to retain the traditional system of points and percentages can also take steps to ensure that their grades are meaningful. The first is to carefully scrutinize them. Every decision about assessment and grading changes the end result. Accordingly, grade calculations are never really "objective," especially since music teachers typically do not feel that all of the links in their grading chains are secure. Thus, teachers are wise to acknowledge that grade calculations are inherently flawed. This does not mean that they are useless, but that their purpose is to facilitate teachers' conclusions about student achievement, not supplant them. Teachers should unapologetically overrule The Math whenever it produces an illogical result. Teachers may feel that this approach exposes them to questions about their grades, and indeed this may be true. However, it is difficult to argue that the potential for less complaining is adequate justification for a flawed system, particularly when so much is at stake for students. If grades use a "learning game" structure, then any conversation about grades is inevitably about learning, and few teachers reject conversations with students and families about that.

Teachers using percentages may also consider the effects of three grading policies detailed in Chapter 8: weighting by curricular goals, penalties for

Table 9.4: GRADE FORMULA WITH EXTRA WEIGHT FOR PERFORMING

Grade on Performing standard	Grades on other standards	Final grade (SBG format)	Final grade (letter format)
Proficient performer	PPP	Proficient	A
	PPD	Proficient	A
	PPB	Proficient	A
	PDD	Proficient	A
	PDB	Proficient	A
	PBB	Developing	B
	DDD	Developing	B
	DDB	Developing	B
	DBB	Developing	B
	BBB	Developing	C
Developing performer	PPP	Proficient	A
	PPD	Proficient	A
	PPB	Developing	B
	PDD	Developing	B
	PDB	Developing	B
	PBB	Developing	C
	DDD	Developing	C
	DDB	Developing	C
	DBB	Developing	C
	BBB	Beginning	D
Beginning performer	PPP	Developing	B
	PPD	Developing	B
	PPB	Developing	C
	PDD	Developing	C
	PDB	Developing	C
	PBB	Beginning	D
	DDD	Developing	C
	DDB	Beginning	D
	DBB	Beginning	D
	BBB	Beginning	F

late and missed work, and the outsized effect of zeros. Percentage grades can still be fair and educational when the grades are based on content mastery, thoughtfully calculated as communication rather than motivation or punishment, and interpreted considering the presence of a sizeable margin of error.

The rest of this chapter is devoted to addressing non-academic factors that commonly arise in music grading.

- "Participation"
- Attendance
- Practice records
- Cherry-picked excerpts
- Extra credit
- "Tough" grading

PARTICIPATION

So-called "class participation" is one of the main reasons that music grades fail to function as unbiased reports of academic achievement. "Participation" is not part of an evaluation of students' musical ability. "Participation" is usually defined and assessed according to the ensemble music teacher's cultural

Example 9.1: Work habits rubric

Classroom habits are strong. You set up quickly, have a pencil, treat equipment respectfully, and keep gum, candy, and food away from our expensive instruments.	Classroom habits are developing. NEXT STEPS:	Classroom habits need improvement. NEXT STEPS:
Responsibility is strong. You remember and take care of your instrument and folder, turn in paperwork on time, and keep your uniform looking sharp.	Responsibility is developing. NEXT STEPS:	Responsibility needs improvement. NEXT STEPS:
Rehearsal focus is strong. You stop playing when the conductor stops, listen when someone is speaking or making music, and study or silently practice when you have the opportunity.	Rehearsal focus is developing. NEXT STEPS:	Rehearsal focus needs improvement. NEXT STEPS:
Attendance is strong. You are present and on time for before-school and after-school commitments.	Attendance is developing. NEXT STEPS:	Attendance needs improvement. NEXT STEPS:
Other comments and Next Steps:		

values and desire for behavior control, practically guaranteeing that subjective judgments influence the grade. All too often, factors such as students' race, gender identity, culture, personality, exceptionality, and socioeconomic status are implicitly or explicitly associated with being a "good kid" or "hard worker," and thus those factors end up reflected in music grades. To be sure, there are certain expectations of membership in a community band, worship choir, and other musical activities students may pursue during or after their time in school ensembles. Teachers can certainly use assessments of work habits or "rehearsal skills" such as Example 9.1 to make students aware of these norms and coach them on their development.

ATTENDANCE

Grading attendance in class and at after-school events has many of the same problems as "participation." Attendance is important, but it is not a curricular outcome. If a student misses a rehearsal or performance, he or she is not a demonstrably worse musician compared with the previous day. Music teachers often argue that concerts are important summative assessments. However, as elaborated in Chapter 7, concerts may be assessments of a group or program, but they are not assessments of individuals. Teachers typically do not evaluate each student's musical accomplishments during the concert. Students are usually graded on non-academic factors such as attendance and attire.

Nearly all students want to be in performances; it is a primary reason that children enroll in music classes. Students whose parents are responsible for their absences, whether because of transportation, caring for a sibling, or a ski vacation, cannot be influenced by a grade. Either the student does what the parents say and is penalized for it by the school, or the parents call the teacher and make up a story to get the absence excused. As much as teachers want to present a polished performance, attendance is still not an academic outcome. Teachers can emphasize concerts, describe them as "mandatory" in the handbook, proactively contact parents, and urge students to attend because their peers are counting on them while still excluding concert attendance from grade calculations.

Attire is a similar situation. Students with the means to acquire black socks will almost always wear them because black socks are the expectation, not because of a potential grade deduction. Even for teachers who believe that there must be "consequences" for mistakes, embarrassment about wearing the wrong socks in public is consequence enough. Students who are worried about consequences for shoes or arriving late are not poised to perform their best. Teachers who believe in punishments for concert infractions might consider how much disruption any of this actually causes and whether the disruption merits the lasting harm low grades can cause for students.

Thoughtful educators may also be able to work with their school administration to handle absences from concerts and rehearsals through the school's existing attendance policy. Skipping an evening rehearsal would then carry the same implications as skipping a class meeting; there may be repercussions, but not in the academic grade report. As a bonus, if the concert is a privilege and not for a grade, then teachers can use it as an incentive (e.g., "You may have unlimited retakes, but you can only perform if you have at least a B on all of your singing tests"). Teachers who do not permit students to perform and still reduce a grade should consider the fairness of this practice carefully, as should those who require busy work as a "make-up" for missing a performance.

PRACTICE RECORDS AND HOMEWORK

By definition, practice is formative assessment and should be excluded from grade calculations. The benefits of a certain required amount of practice are questionable in any case. Different students take different amounts of time to develop certain abilities, and wise teachers are well aware that quantity of practice does not mean quality, or even minimal productivity. As professionals, we are judged by outputs, not inputs. Becoming a lawyer requires a passing score on the bar exam, not a certain amount of time studying. College music programs work the same way—the audition is assessed, not the work that went into it. The expectation is the amount of practice that will get the job done.

Therefore, teachers should consider engaging students in regular assessment of performance, not practice. Students who are expected to meet a performance standard will either practice until they meet it, meet it without home practice, or not meet it and need to practice for their required retake. This has the effect of compelling students to actually make music after school instead of merely obtaining or forging a parent signature. (*I admit it; I faked some of my practice cards in middle school. Sorry, Mom and Dad.*) It also sends the "learning game" message that what matters is the product, not the amount of process. Research has shown that students who are merely told to "go practice" spend most of their practice time aimlessly.[6] Teachers who provide specific goals for practice or promote metacognition with practice logs such as Example 9.2 can expect better results even without a timer.

Example 9.2: Sample practice log

What I played at home this week			
Categories:	TE = Technical exercises	OM = Orchestra music	JF = Just for fun!
Day	Category	What did you play?	What did you accomplish? What work remains?
_____	_____	_____	_____
_____	_____	_____	_____
_____	_____	_____	_____

Homework is also a type of formative practice. Teachers may wish to record homework completion without assigning a grade, or require homework completion as a condition of, for example, a test retake. Some teachers also give a short "homework quiz" at the beginning of class—one or two questions that utilize the skills from the homework assignment. This eliminates the incentive to copy homework, as copying doesn't help on the quiz.

OTHER CONSIDERATIONS

Cherry-picked excerpts

Music educators select repertoire that will be technically and musically accessible for most students, making it difficult enough to challenge advanced performers and acknowledging that it will be a stretch for some. Music educators also often select the most difficult sections from a piece of repertoire for singing or playing tests in order to motivate students to practice them. Teachers who wish to grade concert repertoire excerpts should realize that, if they select the difficult sections, they are only assessing a fraction of the music on the program, most of which all students can perform without difficulty. A student who performs poorly on the most difficult 10 percent of the repertoire has probably still succeeded with the untested 90 percent. While teachers using SBG can account for this when considering performing mastery, it will distort percentages. An excerpt grading scale of 10, 9, 8, Redo is more valid than the traditional 1–10. They can also intermittently test students on excerpts with which they expect them to succeed. Alternately, if the teacher is confident that each student is able to perform a particular section or excerpt, she can just enter a score in the grade book.

If the 10, 9, 8, Redo scale is used, students will likely be involved in retaking music tests. For music educators who desire a philosophy of continuous improvement, this is a positive outcome. The teacher may establish a deadline, such as two weeks before the concert, for students to pass all repertoire checks. If any sections are beyond a student's current abilities, the teacher may use his or her discretion about whether to simplify, rewrite, or, as a last undesirable option, turn a few measures into a *tacet*. Far from being upset by part editing, students are usually relieved.

Extra credit

Extra credit is by definition a grade bestowed upon a student as a result of a behavior or performance that is external to meeting academic expectations. Extra credit advances the idea that the purpose of school is the grading game of earning points rather than hitting learning targets. Behavior-focused extra credit such as booster meeting attendance or exceeding fundraising goals distorts grades by the including non-academic factors and advantages students whose families are able to contribute. Extra credit for private lesson participation is unjust when some students can easily afford lessons while others cannot, and it is essentially grading practice. A well-designed assessment system should be able to capture the effects of private instruction on students' musical ability. Private lessons, booster participation, attending outside concerts, and fundraising are central to many music programs and should be promoted by all justifiable means. The issue is that their inclusion in grades makes the grading system inequitable and less valid.

Being a "tough grader"

Some teachers pride themselves on the poor grades they assign to students, using harsh grading practices to "send a message" about expectations. While high expectations are laudable, there are many ways to communicate them. Capriciously assigning low grades to students is not a sign of musical or professional integrity. One way to interpret a low grade is that the teacher was unsuccessful with that particular student. Astute educators might also consider the effects that such policies might have on student retention and confidence. To build self-efficacy, teachers are wise to begin the year with assessments designed to help students establish an early pattern of success. Fairness is more important than "toughness." This chapter closes where it began: bad grades are bad motivators!

SUMMARY

Even though they are rarely scrutinized, music grading practices often have room for improvement. Justifiable grades require sound curriculum, learning targets, assessment, evaluation, and grading policies. Music grades are often intended to compel certain behaviors. Standards-based grading practices and careful attention to the role of participation, attendance, and practice records contribute to the core function of communicating students' musicianship.

ACTIVITIES

9.1. Develop power standards and relative weights for an ensemble music class in your performance area.

9.2. Acquire one or more ensemble grading policies or handbooks. Evaluate them in light of the recommendations in Chapters 8 and 9.

9.3. Make a list of positive and negative behaviors that commonly affect "participation" grades. What patterns do you see? What is the profile of a "good kid" that emerges?

9.4. If you have previously assigned grades, take a past semester's assessment information and manipulate grade weights to see how the final grades change. Whose grades go up when content is 100 percent, and whose grade goes down? What changes result from attendance or participation being removed?

SECTION FOUR
Onward

CHAPTER 10

Beginning Your Own Journey

When we plant a rose seed in the earth, we notice that it is small, but we don't criticize it as "rootless and stemless." We treat it as a seed, giving it the water and nourishment required of a seed. When it first shoots up out of the earth, we don't condemn it as being immature and underdeveloped; nor do we criticize the buds for not being open when they appear. We stand in wonder at the process taking place and give the plant the care it needs at each stage of its development. The rose is a rose from the time it is a seed to the time it dies. Within it, at all times, it contains its whole potential. It seems to be constantly in the process of change; yet at each state, at each moment, it is perfectly all right as it is.

W. Timothy Gallwey[1]

Box 10.1: CHAPTER 10 ESSENTIAL QUESTIONS

1. How do the ideas from this book fit together?
2. How can instructional technology help with classroom assessment?
3. What first steps can teachers take to begin using assessment in their music rooms?

DEVELOPING AND USING ASSESSMENTS

Assessment is a continuous process of gathering, evaluating, and acting on information to benefit student learning. Some writers even bristle at the use of the plural "assessments," noting that assessment is not a series of unconnected outside interruptions to teaching but rather an ongoing and integral aspect of it, hopefully frequent enough that neither teacher nor students bat an eye when it occurs. Once assessment is viewed as a process

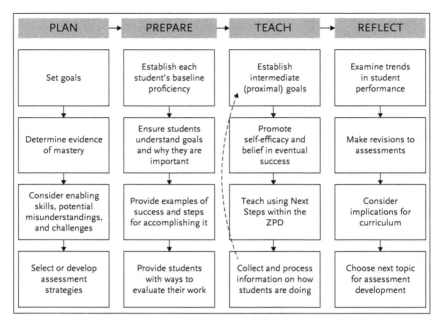

PLAN	PREPARE	TEACH	REFLECT
Set goals	Establish each student's baseline proficiency	Establish intermediate (proximal) goals	Examine trends in student performance
Determine evidence of mastery	Ensure students understand goals and why they are important	Promote self-efficacy and belief in eventual success	Make revisions to assessments
Consider enabling skills, potential misunderstandings, and challenges	Provide examples of success and steps for accomplishing it	Teach using Next Steps within the ZPD	Consider implications for curriculum
Select or develop assessment strategies	Provide students with ways to evaluate their work	Collect and process information on how students are doing	Choose next topic for assessment development

Figure 10.1: Developing and using assessments

rather than an event, there is less pressure for any single act of collecting information to be perfect or comprehensive. There is always tomorrow.

Some subjects are awash in classroom-ready quality assessment ideas. However, using assessment in music education is often more a matter of developing an assessment tool than selecting one. One good process for creating assessments begins with gathering and analyzing a variety of student work samples according to emergent criteria. Groupings may emerge; these are rubric levels and indicators. Common mistakes and feedback suggest relevant enabling skills for advance instruction. After use and revision, teachers will possess tools customized for their own classrooms. The precise tool or method is less important than the mentality underlying it. Any single assessment, or even ongoing data collection, does not improve student learning. For maximum effectiveness, assessment and the resulting insights must be integrated into everyday classroom instruction. Figure 10.1 summarizes the processes involved.

Plan

The first step is to be specific about what students should know or be able to do[2] and to communicate that information to students in a way that they understand: *I want each of my students to know _____ or be able to _____. The goal is defined by evidence of mastery: I want to see each of my students __ __ or _____, but if I see _____ then I'll know that those individuals aren't there yet.* Teachers can also consider the most probable challenges students may face: enabling skills or understandings, or ways that students are likely to struggle. Then, the teacher can select or design assessment tasks and tools to evaluate student progress: *the most efficient ways for me to find out which students can _____ would be to _____.* The teacher may also consider assessment strategies to anticipate which students will face the difficulties identified. Crafting summative assessment materials during the planning stage enables the teacher to ensure that instruction addresses all of the desired skills and understandings. It is also worthwhile to revise concluding activities as they draw near so they align with students' experiences.

Prepare

Students can best accomplish goals that they understand: targets they can see. Demystifying success and how to achieve it is crucial. In order for students to be active participants in learning, they must be able to answer questions such as *What am I supposed to do?* and *How can I best do it?* Students can evaluate their own work and their peers' work when they are taught to do so: *How will I know if I'm on the right track?* Providing the reasoning underpinning the learning goals helps students focus their efforts and is an essential motivator. One of the most common reasons that students don't learn something is that they give up trying to learn it. Students often wonder: *Can I really learn this? Is it worth the effort? What if I fail in front of my friends?* Teachers' attention to these attitudes is critical.

Teach

With the groundwork laid, differentiated instruction is within reach. Familiar pedagogical strategies are more likely to work when the teacher knows what to teach and to whom. Lesson plans can include a range of specific teaching approaches corresponding with assessment results during the class. Metacognitive strategies enable students to be active participants in their learning. Teachers who avoid stigmatizing early failures and promote self-efficacy and growth mindset can help alleviate students' fears and guide them toward accomplishing goals they might not have even attempted in a less supportive environment.

Many lesson plan templates include a section for assessment at the bottom. This is hardly a recipe for integrating formative assessment into instruction. Assessment-focused instructional planning begins with outcomes, followed by evidence of learning and assessments, and only then the procedures and materials. Insert citation to Wiggins & McTighe, Understanding by Design, cited in Chapter 2. Each outcome should have some sort of assessment beyond a casual impression of whether the instruction was successful. Ongoing informal assessment such as "Teacher will assess students' posture throughout the lesson" may not always need to be included; teachers can notice and address posture whether it is in the lesson plan or not. Ongoing posture assessment is certainly insufficient as the only type of assessment in a lesson plan. All items in the Assessment section should also be represented in the Procedures section. If it's worth taking the time to craft an assessment, it's worth considering how it fits into the flow of the class. Planning is where integration of instruction and assessment happens. I am aware that few experienced teachers generate a formal lesson plan from standards to procedures for each class, myself included. However, assessment does require forethought to be maximally effective, even if it's written on the back of a fundraiser envelope.

Reflect

Reflection on new assessments and units nearly always yields possibilities for improvement in the future. Unclear directions, typos, technology issues, advance preparation needs, questions that should have been asked but weren't, questions students found confusing, and completion time are only a few areas to consider noting or revising so that the next time goes more smoothly. Editing materials during a unit—even immediately after a class, or during an afterschool grading session—ensures that everything is ready whenever it is needed in the future. Keeping notes not only on the assessment but also on the instruction is vital. Assessment results usually have implications for curriculum and instruction. Reflecting on enabling skills and understandings, during or after a unit or concert cycle, is particularly productive.

Teachers can gather information about their assessments from many sources. Assessment software, a spreadsheet, or simple observation can reveal which elements of an assessment presented the most difficulty and whether any patterns exist (e.g., many students chose the same distractor). Of interest is whether the issue was with the question or task itself or instruction on the learning that it was designed to represent. While certainly not necessary, software that performs item analysis can, for example, flag test questions that were uncorrelated with most students' overall performance. Teachers can also solicit student feedback and provide space for it in written assessment or when students submit commentary alongside performance tasks or projects. Fellow teachers are also invaluable sounding boards; it will probably take only a few minutes for a colleague to complete most assessments and offer a few suggestions. The inevitable process of revision is another reminder that assessment results are far from being exact and infallible. In illogical or unclear cases, students deserve the benefit of the doubt.

USING TECHNOLOGY

Instructional technology overview

Technology platforms open exciting new avenues for implementing classroom assessment, but they are tools, not magic. If used thoughtlessly, they are no better than traditional classroom activities. Technology comes with its own limitations. In their excitement to use it, teachers can fail to consider the ways it can restrict assessment methods and fundamentally alter learning activities (discussed in Chapter 1). In particular, technology makes selected-response assessment so easy that it can crowd out other methods. Even if it may appear that all children inherently know how to use technology, this is not the case, especially for students living in poverty. Finally, educators must grapple with pressing questions about students' data security, exposure to targeted advertising, and privacy.

Decisions about which platforms to use are affected by many factors, including what is provided (and prohibited) by the school district and a fast-changing marketplace. Even as many districts are beginning to provide students with tablets or laptops, access is an issue of equity in most schools. Still, it would be foolish to ignore the potential of technology to facilitate data collection, evaluation, and feedback. Many of the following recommendations work with smartphones, tablets, laptops, and home desktop computers, but this is not always the case. A school IT specialist will probably be eager to assist with specifics and also district policies, which must be followed to the letter.

Current platforms

The most comprehensive kind of instructional technology is a learning management system (LMS). An LMS is usually a collection of tools for managing assignments, grades, and more. They often feature built-in tools for handling online quizzes (even self-grading), written assignments, and media files such as audio or video of individual performance. There are many commercial learning management systems; readers may be familiar with names like Blackboard, Canvas, Google Classroom, Haiku, Infinite Campus, or Schoology. School districts often purchase these platforms for all teachers and students, and student familiarity can be an important asset.

There are also apps and websites that simulate flash cards such as StudyBlue and Quizlet, many of which allow pictures or audio files as questions. Quick tools for capturing student responses include Kahoot and Poll Everywhere, while Socrative and Quizalize offer more functionality such as self-grading quizzes and reports. Apps such as Plickers enable phone cameras to capture student responses on cards they hold up. Subscription services such as SmartMusic can evaluate performance tasks according to basic criteria. Districts may subscribe to an assessment management service, which may allow teachers to see whole-class and individual progress reports down to the rubric criterion. The website musictheory.net and corresponding Tenuto and Clef Tutor apps offer customizable exercises for a variety of music theory and literacy concepts. Other music apps and websites include ReadRhythm, NinGenius, BandBlast, Sight-Reading Factory, and countless others. This list is not intended to be comprehensive. There are useful alternatives to everything listed here, and new offerings are continually becoming available. The particular platform is less important than its thoughtful use.

Fancy technology is not necessary. Free websites such as Google Forms can be used for submitting quiz responses, and there are innumerable ways to transfer media files. Teachers could also make a spreadsheet to quickly enter scores or brief typed comments and then use mail merge to turn them into a form to hand to students. Computers and mobile devices have built-in recording software that facilitates sharing audio or video files. The music teacher does not need to figure this out alone. Colleagues, administrators, and instructional coaches can usually help. Bill Bauer's book *Music Learning Today*[3] has many practical ideas as well.

GETTING STARTED WITH ASSESSMENT IN YOUR TEACHING

Ensemble teachers looking for ways to start using more varied assessment practices are primed to do so. Assessment is already woven into the fabric of music instruction. There is no need to Do Formative Assessment all at once. Experiment; try a few new things; gain experience with the process; gradually refine and broaden what you are doing. To use a baseball analogy, batters who try to swing hard and hit a home run often strike out. Your

- List critical enabling skills that come up frequently in class.
- Frame learning through the AfL questions.
- Create checklists and rubrics for efficient formal formative assessment of fundamentals.
- Experiment with formal PPA.
- Use QFATs to check for understanding.
- Involve students in self and peer evaluation.
- Promote growth mindset.
- Reconsider grading policies.
- Consult with a peer or instructional coach.

assessment journey will likely be most successful with a series of singles. You will be learning how to teach in new ways. Don't forget about your *own* metacognition, ZPD, and growth mindset.

The purpose of classroom assessment is to enhance instruction that is already happening. Music teachers don't have time for a new obligation that takes time away from their existing goals; there isn't enough class time for the things they are already doing. Therefore, the best place to start (Box 10.2) may be a concept or skill that the teacher already values and teaches. Box 10.3 contains guiding questions to help you think through the information you are seeking and the best ways to find it.

New assessment strategies do not have to mean new, extraneous curricular material. Over time, though, assessment may lead to curricular evolution. Assessment results often reveal patterns of enabling skills that students need to improve. Incorporating such concepts into the curriculum benefits current and future students. This is not an admission of failure on the teacher's part. It is data-informed instruction in the most helpful sense.

Music education is not the only field undergoing a paradigm shift with respect to assessment, meaning that opportunities for collaboration are abundant. Administrators and instructional coaches are usually assets, but may be hindered by their many competing pressures and frequent lack of music expertise. Connections can be made with other like-minded music educators locally, in professional organizations, or through social media. Resources and ideas from general education are also helpful. As is always the case in education, some methods and advice are misguided or designed to sell a particular product. In the same way that buying and wearing a fitness tracker does not make you healthy, the benefits of classroom

---

Box 10.3: GUIDING QUESTIONS FOR ASSESSMENT PLANNING

- What is my learning target?
- Is this a Knowledge, Reasoning, Skill, Product, or Disposition target?
- What enabling skills or background information will students need?
- How are students possible or likely to struggle?
- What information am I hoping that assessment will provide?
- What task(s) will highlight this information?
- What assessment method(s) will help to accurately and efficiently record student performance?
- What feedback am I likely to give?
- How will I communicate assessment results?
- What are my Next Steps if students are doing well?
- What are my Next Steps if students are struggling?

---

assessment come from intentional and fundamental changes to teaching practice, not any particular nomenclature, method, or technology.

AN OPPORTUNITY FOR CHANGE IN MUSIC EDUCATION

The music educators I have encountered in my travels are overwhelmingly hard-working, selfless, caring people who sincerely want to do what's best for their students. There are many ways to do right by students: lending a sympathetic ear, offering extra help after school, and heartfelt expressions of gratitude or congratulations. There is yet another way to do right by students that is so evident that we often overlook it: curriculum, instruction, assessment, and classroom policies that promote musical understanding, self-efficacy, self-worth, inclusion, equity, and dignity. Whether it is due to tradition, lack of expertise, or just teachers feeling overwhelmed, music education has room for growth in these areas. The children in our care do not always feel more like a budding rose than a cog in the wheel of "the program." I did not set out to write this book because I believe in assessment, although I do. I wrote this book because I care about children, young musicians, students—mine and yours. Let our instructional improvements be motivated not by trophies and plaques, state legislatures and insistent administrators, or reflexive adherence to "tradition," but by the diverse, imperfect, unfinished, wonderfully unique students we are committed to serving.

SUMMARY

Using assessment well involves integrating it into the regular affairs of the classroom. By following a process of Plan, Prepare, Teach, and Reflect, teachers can maximize the effectiveness of their assessment practices. A plethora of options for using education technology opens doors but also requires the educator to learn and vet each platform. Learning how to use assessment is an ongoing process, just like learning anything else. Teachers are wise to assess outcomes they already teach and value and gradually improve and expand their assessment practices. There will inevitably be Through first steps, inevitable missteps, and next steps, the benefits for students will make the endeavor worthwhile.

ACTIVITIES

10.1. Choose a class, real or hypothetical. Pick a skill or concept and describe how you might implement the steps in Figure 10.1 to teach it to students.

10.2. List the instructional technology with which you are familiar or that is frequently used in your school district. Note what learning target types and assessment methods it handles best. Share your list with peers and identify any trends in types and methods you see.

10.3. Review your responses to the activities from previous chapters. Journal about what jumps out at you.

10.4. Write about your own Next Steps with regard to classroom assessment. How can you incorporate it into the teaching you are doing now, and how could you use it in the future?

NOTES

CHAPTER 1

1. Grant P. Wiggins, *Educative Assessment* (San Francisco, CA: Jossey-Bass, 1998), 7.
2. Robert J. Marzano, *What Works in Schools: Translating Research into Action* (Alexandria, VA: ASCD, 2003); Robert J. Marzano, *The Art and Science of Teaching: A Comprehensive Framework for Effective Instruction* (Alexandria, VA: ASCD, 2007); Robert J. Marzano, *Formative Assessment and Standards-Based Grading* (Bloomington, IN: Solution Tree, 2009); Michael C. Rodriguez, "The Role of Classroom Assessment in Student Performance on TIMSS," *Applied Measurement in Education* 17, no. 1 (2004): 1–24; Rick Stiggins and Jan Chappuis, "Using Student-Involved Classroom Assessment to Close Achievement Gaps," *Theory Into Practice* 44, no. 1 (2005): 11–18, doi:10.1207/s15430421tip4401_3; Dylan Wiliam et al., "Teachers Developing Assessment for Learning: Impact on Student Achievement," *Assessment in Education* 11, no. 1 (2004): 49–65, doi:10.1080/0969594042000208994; Paul Black and Dylan Wiliam, "'In Praise of Educational Research': Formative Assessment," *British Educational Research Journal* 29, no. 5 (2003): 623–37, doi:10.1080/0141192032000133721.
3. e.g., Gary E. McPherson, "From Child to Musician: Skill Development during the Beginning Stages of Learning an Instrument," *Psychology of Music* 33, no. 1 (2005): 5–35, doi:10.1177/0305735605048012; Susan Hallam, *Music Psychology in Education* (London: Institute of Education, University of London, 2006).
4. Rick Wormeli, *Fair Isn't Always Equal: Assessing and Grading in the Differentiated Classroom* (Portland, ME: Stenhouse, 2006).
5. Scott C. Shuler, "Music Assessment, Part 2: Instructional Improvement and Teacher Evaluation," *Music Educators Journal* 98, no. 3 (2012): 7–10; W. James Popham, *Classroom Assessment: What Teachers Need to Know* (Boston: Allyn & Bacon, 2008).
6. Randall Everett Allsup and Cathy Benedict, "The Problems of Band: An Inquiry into the Future of Instrumental Music Education," *Philosophy of Music Education Review* 16, no. 2 (2008): 156–73.
7. Jane W. Davidson, Michael J. Howe, and John A. Sloboda, "Environmental Factors in the Development of Musical Performance Skill over the Life Span," in *The Social Psychology of Music*, ed. David Hargreaves and Adrian North (New York: Oxford University Press, 1997), 188–208; Michael J. A. Howe, Jane W. Davidson, and John A. Sloboda, "Innate Talents: Reality or Myth?," *Behavioral and Brain Sciences* 21, no. 3 (1998): 399–442, doi:10.1017/S0140525X9800123X; Andreas C. Lehmann, John A. Sloboda, and Robert H. Woody, *Psychology for*

Musicians: Understanding and Acquiring the Skills (New York: Oxford University Press, 2006).

8. Rick Stiggins, *Revolutionize Assessment* (Thousand Oaks, CA: Corwin, 2014).

9. Janet E. Coffey et al., "The Missing Disciplinary Substance of Formative Assessment," *Journal of Research in Science Teaching* 48, no. 10 (2011): 1128.

10. L. S. Vygotskiĭ, *Mind in Society: The Development of Higher Psychological Processes*, trans. Michael Cole (Cambridge, MA: Harvard University Press, 1978).

11. David Wood, Jerome S. Bruner, and Gail Ross, "The Role of Tutoring in Problem Solving," *Journal of Child Psychology and Psychiatry, and Allied Disciplines* 17, no. 2 (1976): 89–100.

12. Joseph A. Durlak et al., "The Impact of Enhancing Students' Social and Emotional Learning: A Meta-Analysis of School-Based Universal Interventions," *Child Development* 82, no. 1 (2011): 405–32, doi:10.1111/j.1467-8624.2010.01564.x; Rebecca D. Taylor et al., "Promoting Positive Youth Development Through School-Based Social and Emotional Learning Interventions: A Meta-Analysis of Follow-Up Effects," *Child Development* 88, no. 4 (2017).

13. Albert Bandura, "Self-Efficacy: Toward a Unifying Theory of Behavioral Change," *Psychological Review* 84, no. 2 (1977): 191–215, doi:10.1037/0033-295X.84.2.191; Frank Pajares and Dale Schunk, "Self-Beliefs and School Success: Self-Efficacy, Self-Concept, and School Achievement," in *Self Perception*, ed. R. J. Riding and S. G. Raynor (Westport, CT: Ablex, 2001), 239–65.

14. Paul Black and Dylan Wiliam, "Inside the Black Box: Raising Standards through Classroom Assessment," *Phi Delta Kappan* 80, no. 2 (1998): 87.

15. John Pryor and Barbara Crossouard, "A Socio-Cultural Theorisation of Formative Assessment," *Oxford Review of Education* 34, no. 1 (2008): 1–20; Lauren Kapalka Richerme, "Measuring Music Education: A Philosophical Investigation of the Model Cornerstone Assessments," *Journal of Research in Music Education* 64, no. 3 (2016): 274–93, doi:10.1177/0022429416659250.

16. Alfie Kohn, "Schooling beyond Measure," *Education Week*, September 19, 2012, 36.

17. Gipps, "Socio-Cultural Aspects of Assessment," 370.

18. I will use "exceptionality" as an umbrella term to refer to students with disabilities, students identified as gifted, students with special learning needs, or a combination of these.

CHAPTER 2

1. Of course, another way to craft a curriculum is to involve students in a collaborative determination of what they would like to learn about music and what musical materials might be best suited for the task. While this approach is highly desirable for many reasons, this discussion of curriculum and assessment begins with the premise that the teacher has certain goals in mind.

2. Grant P. Wiggins and Jay McTighe, *Understanding by Design*, 2nd ed. (Alexandria, VA: ASCD, 2005).

3. National Association for Music Education, "Core Music Standards," 2014, 3, http://www.nafme.org/my-classroom/standards/core-music-standards/.

4. Virginia Department of Education, "Music Standards of Learning," 2013, 68, http://www.doe.virginia.gov/testing/sol/standards_docs/fine_arts/2013/music/std_finearts_music.pdf.

5. Jan Chappuis et al., *Classroom Assessment for Student Learning*, 2nd ed. (Upper Saddle River, NJ: Pearson, 2012), 42.
6. Wiggins and McTighe, *Understanding by Design*, 59.
7. Chappuis et al., *Classroom Assessment for Student Learning*.
8. Jan Chappuis, *Seven Strategies of Assessment for Learning*, 2nd ed. (Hoboken, NJ: Pearson, 2015), 35.
9. Caroline V. Gipps, *Beyond Testing: Towards a Theory of Educational Assessment* (Bristol, PA: Falmer, 1994); Dylan Wiliam and Siobhán Leahy, *Embedding Formative Assessment: Practical Techniques for K–12 Classrooms* (West Palm Beach, FL: Learning Sciences International, 2015).

CHAPTER 3

1. Alfie Kohn, "The Case against Grades," *Educational Leadership* 69, no. 3 (2011): 28.
2. Paul Black and Dylan Wiliam, "The Formative Purpose: Assessment Must First Promote Learning," *Yearbook of the National Society for the Study of Education* 103, no. 2 (2005): 21–22, doi:10.1111/j.1744-7984.2004.tb00047.x.
3. Thomas R. Guskey and Lee Ann Jung, *Answers to Essential Questions about Standards, Assessments, Grading, and Reporting* (Thousand Oaks, CA: Corwin, 2013), 39.
4. Thomas R. Guskey, "Using Assessments to Improve Teaching and Learning," in *Ahead of the Curve: The Power of Assessment to Transform Teaching and Learning*, ed. Douglas Reeves (Bloomington, IN: Solution Tree, 2007), 22–23.
5. Jan Chappuis, *Seven Strategies of Assessment for Learning*, 2nd ed. (Hoboken, NJ: Pearson, 2015), 12, adapted from J. Myron Atkin, Paul Black, and Janet Coffey, eds., *Classroom Assessment and the National Science Education Standards* (Washington, DC: National Academy Press, 2001).
6. Rick Stiggins, "Assessment for Learning: An Essential Foundation of Productive Instruction," in *Ahead of the Curve: The Power of Assessment to Transform Teaching and Learning*, ed. Douglas Reeves (Bloomington, IN: Solution Tree, 2007), 62.
7. Grant P. Wiggins, *Educative Assessment* (San Francisco, CA: Jossey-Bass, 1998), 139.
8. Guskey, "Using Assessments to Improve Teaching and Learning," 17; Rick Wormeli, *Fair Isn't Always Equal: Assessing and Grading in the Differentiated Classroom* (Portland, ME: Stenhouse, 2006).
9. Janet E. Coffey et al., "The Missing Disciplinary Substance of Formative Assessment," *Journal of Research in Science Teaching* 48, no. 10 (2011): 1109–36.
10. W. James Popham, *Classroom Assessment: What Teachers Need to Know* (Boston: Allyn & Bacon, 2008); Judith A. Arter and Jan Chappuis, *Creating and Recognizing Quality Rubrics* (Portland, OR: ETS, 2006).
11. Robert J. Marzano, *Transforming Classroom Grading* (Alexandria, VA: Association for Supervision and Curriculum Development, 2000).
12. Mary L. Cohen, "Writing between Rehearsals: A Tool for Assessment and Building Camaraderie," *Music Educators Journal* 98, no. 3 (2012): 43–48, doi:10.1177/0027432111434743.
13. Jan Chappuis et al., *Classroom Assessment for Student Learning*, 2nd ed. (Upper Saddle River, NJ: Pearson, 2012), 364.
14. Alice M. Hammel and Ryan M. Hourigan, *Teaching Music to Students with Special Needs: A Label-Free Approach*, 2nd ed. (New York: Oxford University Press, 2017).

15. Lee Ann Jung and Thomas R. Guskey, *Grading Exceptional and Struggling Learners* (Thousand Oaks, CA: Corwin, 2011).

CHAPTER 4

1. Ken O'Connor, *How to Grade for Learning, K–12*, 3rd ed. (Thousand Oaks, CA: Corwin, 2009), 126.
2. John Hattie and Helen Timperley, "The Power of Feedback," *Review of Educational Research* 77, no. 1 (2007): 81–112, doi:10.3102/003465430298487.
3. Dylan Wiliam, "The Secret of Effective Feedback," *Educational Leadership* 73, no. 7 (2016): 13.
4. Dylan Wiliam and Siobhán Leahy, *Embedding Formative Assessment: Practical Techniques for K–12 Classrooms* (West Palm Beach, FL: Learning Sciences International, 2015), 40.
5. Peter Johnson, "Performance as Experience: The Problem of Assessment Criteria," *British Journal of Music Education* 14, no. 3 (1997): 271–82; Michael Stanley, Ron Brooker, and Ross Gilbert, "Examiner Perceptions of Using Criteria in Music Performance Assessment," *Research Studies in Music Education* 18, no. 1 (2002): 46–56, doi:10.1177/1321103X020180010601; D. Royce Sadler, "Indeterminacy in the Use of Preset Criteria for Assessment and Grading," *Assessment & Evaluation in Higher Education* 34, no. 2 (2009): 159–79, doi:10.1080/02602930801956059.
6. Daniel Deutsch, "Authentic Assessment in Music Composition: Feedback That Facilitates Creativity," *Music Educators Journal* 102, no. 3 (2016): 53–59, doi:10.1177/0027432115621608.
7. Diana Blom and John Encarnacao, "Student-Chosen Criteria for Peer Assessment of Tertiary Rock Groups in Rehearsal and Performance: What's Important?," *British Journal of Music Education* 29, no. 1 (2012): 25–43; Anne Davies, "Involving Students in the Classroom Assessment Process," in *Ahead of the Curve: The Power of Assessment to Transform Teaching and Learning*, ed. Douglas Reeves (Bloomington, IN: Solution Tree, 2007), 31–58.
8. Janet Mills, "Assessing Musical Performance Musically," *Educational Studies* 17, no. 2 (1991): 173–81, doi:10.1080/0305569910170206.
9. Stanley, Brooker, and Gilbert, "Examiner Perceptions of Using Criteria"; Sadler, "Indeterminacy in the Use of Preset Criteria."
10. Thomas R. Guskey, "Why the Label 'Exceeds Standard' Doesn't Work," *Education Week*, October 17, 2014, http://blogs.edweek.org/edweek/finding_common_ground/2014/10/why_the_label_exceeds_standard_doesnt_work.html.
11. Susan B. Neuman, "The Danger of Data-Driven Instruction," *Educational Leadership* 74, no. 3 (2016): 24–29.
12. Wiliam and Leahy, *Embedding Formative Assessment*.

CHAPTER 5

1. Joseph L. Casey, *Teaching Techniques and Insights for Instrumental Music Educators*, rev.ed. (Chicago: GIA, 1991), 467.
2. It turns out that transfer isn't as straightforward as many educators would like it to be—that skills and understandings are almost always context-specific. Rather than being discouraging, this fact should instead lead us to redouble our efforts to teach core principles explicitly.

3. Daniel Deutsch, "Authentic Assessment in Music Composition: Feedback That Facilitates Creativity," *Music Educators Journal* 102, no. 3 (2016): 53–59, doi:10.1177/0027432115621608.

4. Maud Hickey, *Music Outside the Lines: Ideas for Composing in K–12 Music Classrooms* (New York: Oxford University Press, 2012).

5. Maud Hickey, "Assessment Rubrics for Music Composition," *Music Educators Journal* 85, no. 4 (1999): 26–33, doi:10.2307/3399530.

CHAPTER 6

1. Catherine Larsen, "Interview with Larry Rachleff: The Heart and Brain in Performing," in *Performing with Understanding: The Challenge of the National Standards for Music Education*, ed. Bennett Reimer (Reston, VA: MENC, 2000), 142.

2. Sheila Scott, "Evaluating Tasks for Performance-Based Assessments: Advice for Music Teachers," *General Music Today* 17, no. 2 (2004): 17–27.

CHAPTER 7

1. Mitchell Robinson, "The Inchworm and the Nightingale: On the (Mis)use of Data in Music Teacher Evaluation," *Arts Education Policy Review* 116, no. 1 (2015): 9–21; Phillip M. Hash, "Large-Group Contest Ratings and Music Teacher Evaluation: Issues and Recommendations," *Arts Education Policy Review* 114, no. 4 (2013): 163–69, doi:10.1080/10632913.2013.826035.

2. Ramona M. Wis, *The Conductor as Leader: Principles of Leadership Applied to Life on the Podium* (Chicago: GIA, 2007), 69–70.

3. Robert A. Duke, "Measures of Instructional Effectiveness in Music Research," *Bulletin of the Council for Research in Music Education* 143 (Winter 1999/2000): 1–48; Robert A. Duke, "Bringing the Art of Rehearsal into Focus: The Rehearsal Frame as a Model for Prescriptive Analysis of Rehearsal Conducting," *Journal of Band Research* 30, no. 1 (1994): 78–95.

4. Gary E. McPherson, "From Child to Musician: Skill Development during the Beginning Stages of Learning an Instrument," *Psychology of Music* 33, no. 1 (2005): 5–35, doi:10.1177/0305735605048012.

5. Santa, Carol M., Lynn T. Havens, and Bonnie J. Valdes. *Project CRISS: Creating Independence through Student-Owned Strategies*. Dubuque, IA: Kendall/Hunt, 2004.

6. Teachers are encouraged to consult Brent Edstrom, *Recording on a Budget: How to Make Great Audio Recordings without Breaking the Bank* (New York: Oxford University Press, 2011).

CHAPTER 8

1. Jane Bailey and Jay McTighe, "Reporting Achievement at the Secondary Level: What and How," in *Communicating Student Learning*, ed. Thomas R. Guskey (Alexandria, VA: ASCD, 1996), 2.

2. Thomas R. Guskey and Lee Ann Jung, *Answers to Essential Questions about Standards, Assessments, Grading, and Reporting* (Thousand Oaks, CA: Corwin, 2013), 64.

3. Susan M. Brookhart et al., "A Century of Grading Research: Meaning and Value in the Most Common Educational Measure," *Review of Educational Research* 86, no. 4 (2016): 803–48, doi:10.3102/0034654316672069.

4. Ibid.; Robert J. Marzano, *Transforming Classroom Grading* (Alexandria, VA: Association for Supervision and Curriculum Development, 2000).
5. Ken O'Connor, *How to Grade for Learning, K–12*, 3rd ed. (Thousand Oaks, CA: Corwin, 2009), 16.
6. Jay McTighe and Ken O'Connor, "Seven Practices for Effective Learning," *Educational Leadership* 63, no. 3 (2005): 16.
7. Guskey and Jung, *Answers to Essential Questions*, 80.
8. Edward L. Deci, Richard Koestner, and Richard M. Ryan, "Extrinsic Rewards and Intrinsic Motivation in Education: Reconsidered Once Again," *Review of Educational Research* 71, no. 1 (2001): 1–27, doi:10.3102/00346543071001001; Marylène Gagné and Edward L. Deci, "Self-Determination Theory and Work Motivation," *Journal of Organizational Behavior* 26, no. 4 (2005): 331–62; Alfie Kohn, *Punished by Rewards: The Trouble with Gold Stars, Incentive Plans, A's, Praise, and Other Bribes* (Boston: Houghton Mifflin, 1993).
9. Rick Wormeli, *Fair Isn't Always Equal: Assessing and Grading in the Differentiated Classroom* (Portland, ME: Stenhouse, 2006), 31.
10. Alfie Kohn, "The Case against Grades," *Educational Leadership* 69, no. 3 (2011): 28–33; Alfie Kohn, "Grading: The Issue Is Not How but Why," *Educational Leadership* 52, no. 2 (1994): 38.
11. O'Connor, *School Leader's Guide to Grading*, 2.
12. Alfie Kohn, who advocates the complete elimination of grades, once compared standards-based grading to putting lipstick on a pig. While it is true that there are problems with grading that SBG does not solve, this discussion assumes that the music teacher is required to assign grades to students. Principles of SBG have much to offer in that scenario.
13. Marzano, *Transforming Classroom Grading*.
14. Reporting a grade of "Incomplete" in this situation is an option that is also gaining wider acceptance. However, if the teacher has enough information to make a determination—affirmative or negative—about content mastery even when some assignments are missing, then the corresponding grade is appropriate. The purpose of the assignments is to inform the teachers' judgment of content mastery.
15. Arter and Chappuis, *Creating and Recognizing Quality Rubrics*, 114.
16. O'Connor, "Last Frontier," 139.

CHAPTER 9

1. Joshua A. Russell and James R. Austin, "Assessment Practices of Secondary Music Teachers," *Journal of Research in Music Education* 58, no. 1 (April 1, 2010): 43, doi:10.1177/0022429409360062.
2. E. James Kotora, "Assessment Practices in the Choral Music Classroom: A Survey of Ohio High School Choral Music Teachers and College Choral Methods Professors," *Contributions to Music Education* 32, no. 2 (2005): 65–80; Paul R. Lehman, "Grading Practices in Music," *Music Educators Journal* 84, no. 5 (1998): 37–40, doi:10.2307/3399129.
3. Patricia O'Toole, *Shaping Sound Musicians: An Innovative Approach to Teaching Comprehensive Musicianship through Performance* (Chicago: GIA, 2003), 72.
4. Russell and Austin, "Assessment Practices of Secondary Music Teachers."
5. Colleen Conway and Tom Jeffers, "Parent, Student, and Teacher Perceptions of Assessment Procedures in Beginning Instrumental Music," *Bulletin of the Council for Research in Music Education*, no. 160 (2004): 16–25.

6. Peter Miksza, "The Development of a Measure of Self-Regulated Practice Behavior for Beginning and Intermediate Instrumental Music Students," *Journal of Research in Music Education* 59, no. 4 (2012): 321–38, doi:10.1177/0022429411414717.

CHAPTER 10

1. W. Timothy Gallwey, *The Inner Game of Tennis* (New York: Random House, 1974), 21.
2. While state and national standards are often relevant to classroom curricula and can be a good starting place for a curriculum, teachers need not feel limited to any one list of how students should engage with music.
3. William I. Bauer, *Music Learning Today: Digital Pedagogy for Creating, Performing, and Responding to Music* (New York: Oxford University Press, 2014).

FURTHER READING FOR TEACHERS

Chappuis, Jan. *Seven Strategies of Assessment for Learning.* 2nd ed. Hoboken, NJ: Pearson, 2015.

Chappuis, Jan, Rick Stiggins, Steve Chappuis, and Judith Arter. *Classroom Assessment for Student Learning.* 2nd ed. Upper Saddle River, NJ: Pearson, 2012.

Duke, Robert A. *Intelligent Music Teaching.* Austin, TX: Learning & Behavior Resources, 2005.

Guskey, Thomas R., and Lee Ann Jung. *Answers to Essential Questions about Standards, Assessments, Grading, and Reporting.* Thousand Oaks, CA: Corwin, 2013.

Kohn, Alfie. *Punished by Rewards: The Trouble with Gold Stars, Incentive Plans, A's, Praise, and Other Bribes.* Boston: Houghton Mifflin, 1993.

Marzano, Robert J. *Transforming Classroom Grading.* Alexandria, VA: Association for Supervision and Curriculum Development, 2000.

O'Connor, Ken. *A Repair Kit for Grading: 15 Fixes for Broken Grades.* Boston: Pearson, 2011.

O'Connor, Ken. *How to Grade for Learning: Linking Grades to Standards.* 4th ed. Thousand Oaks, CA: Corwin, 2018.

O'Toole, Patricia. *Shaping Sound Musicians: An Innovative Approach to Teaching Comprehensive Musicianship through Performance.* Chicago, IL: GIA, 2003.

Wiggins, Grant P. *Educative Assessment.* San Francisco, CA: Jossey-Bass, 1998.

Wiggins, Grant P., and Jay McTighe. *Understanding by Design.* 2nd ed. Alexandria, VA: ASCD, 2005.

Wiliam, Dylan, and Siobhán Leahy. *Embedding Formative Assessment: Practical Techniques for K–12 Classrooms.* West Palm Beach, FL: Learning Sciences International, 2015.

Wormeli, Rick. *Fair Isn't Always Equal: Assessment and Grading in the Differentiated Classroom.* 2nd ed. Portland, ME: Stenhouse, 2018.

INDEX